WILDE LIKE US

GREEN BRIDGE GIRLS
BOOK 1

A.K. RITCHIE

WILDE
like us

a.k. ritchie

Important note about this novel:

This book contains depictions and discussions of self-harm, alcohol and drug use, addiction, abandonment, and death of a parent.

Please prioritize your well-being while reading, and consider whether now is the right time to for this story.

This is a work of fiction. Names, characters, places, and incidents either are the product of the author's imagination or are used fictitiously, and any resemblance to actually persons, living or dead, business establishments, events, or locales is entirely coincidental.

Copyright © 2025 by A.K. Ritchie

All rights reserved.

No part of this book may be reproduced in any form or by any electronic or mechanical means, including information storage and retrieval systems, without written permission from the author, except for the use of brief quotations in a book review.

No Training AI: Without in any way limiting the author's [and publisher's] exclusive rights under copyright, any use of this publication to "train" generative artificial intelligence (AI) technologies to generate text is expressly prohibited. The author reserves all rights to license uses of this work for generative AI training and development of machine learning language models.

ISBN 978-1-7779061-6-0

ISBN 978-1-7779061-7-7 (ebook)

CHAPTER ONE

When Harper Wilde walked through the front door of the Swashbuckler, all her friends cheered. It almost helped her forget that her mother hadn't called to wish her a happy birthday again that year.

To make sure nothing ruined her twenty-fifth birthday, Harper Wilde planned every last detail herself. Despite its reputation, she picked the Swashbuckler, the sketchy bar in her neighbourhood, so all of her friends would be able to make it. It took almost a week, but she convinced the owner to let her do bottle service for the night so everyone could drink and have a good time without worrying about money. By the time she finished work, got dressed for a night out, and showed up at the bar, the place was packed with all of her friends.

Olive broke free from the crowd and rushed over. Her purple hair fell in her face as she popped up onto her tiptoes to drape a pink 'Birthday Girl' sash over Harper's head. It had been one of Harper's stipulations not to have birthday signs and banners and balloons. Only Olive could get away with going against Harper's rules. They were like sisters, and

Olive always pushed the rules because she knew Harper would never hold it against her.

"I'm going to let this slide, only because I know how much you hate being in this bar," Harper said, wrapping an arm around Olive's shoulders. Instinctively, Harper's eyes scanned the long wooden bar at the back of the establishment.

A group of six men sat on the stools with their backs to the party that had grown since they arrived. Even in the dim lighting, Harper recognized the faces. They were the same men who hung around out front of the Swashbuckler, smoking cigarettes, and catcalling women who walked by.

None of the people at the bar were Olive's mom, Angelica. Harper would recognize her anywhere.

As she double-checked, she spotted Levi strutting across the bar with a small plastic shot glass in one hand and a beer in the other. He stopped in front of her, his broad chest and shoulders blocking the view of the rest of her friends. She reached up, cupped his face between both of her palms, and smashed her lips against his.

"Too much PDA for me," Olive said with a laugh as she walked away.

When they broke out of their kiss, Levi handed Harper the shot and the beer. He pushed his long, dark hair from his face and said, "Happy birthday, Harper." He stood back and let her take the shot.

The shot of rum burned all the way down in a way that Harper loved. She would miss that feeling as she continued drinking, as all of her senses continued to dull. It was the only feeling she missed as she finished one drink after the other.

"You know, you could have left something for us to do for you," Levi said as Harper took a swig of her beer. "At least I could have made a cake."

Levi had offered to make the cake several times that week, but he'd also spent the week calling his sister and trying to organize things with his cousin to make sure that his parents, who had come down with pneumonia, were being taken care of. Harper didn't want him to worry about her birthday party, and part of her worried that with everything going on with him, she would end up disappointed when he couldn't find the time.

"You look gorgeous," Levi whispered the moment before her friends turned away from the mini dance floor they'd created by pushing tables aside and shouted happy birthday at her.

Harper felt gorgeous. She'd picked out a black dress composed of mostly sheer lace that showed off the tattoos on her arms and legs. However, she'd made sure the opaque black fabric was long enough to cover the ink she'd done on her own upper thighs when learning to tattoo. No one needed to see the uneven lines of Morton Salt Girl or the blown out edges of the crying black heart she did the night she bought her first tattoo machine.

"Why are you not shit-faced yet?" Noah asked as he rolled his wheelchair up next to her. He handed her a shot and said, "I expected you to be stumbling in here."

Harper took the tiny cup he gave her and tapped it against his before they both downed the amber liquid. Noah was one of the two people who owned Silver Sparrow Tattoos, the shop where she had become a professional tattoo artist. Noah and his sister-in-law, Maz, saw Harper drawing on the side of a building with a graffiti marker she found discarded in the alleyway. When she finished, Maz asked her if she ever thought about becoming a tattoo artist. Noah had folded his arms and said he didn't care if she had or not, he could be her apprentice if she stopped graffitiing on the building they'd just bought. It had been Noah who brought her into Silver Sparrow Tattoos and got her out of working the three retail jobs she'd been struggling to maintain. Despite their differences and his lack of patience with her attitude, Noah helped shape her into the artist she had become.

Noah ran a hand over the top of his pale bald head and said, "Happy birthday, kid. If you wanna take the party up a notch, come find me." He winked and tapped the breast pocket of his buffalo plaid shirt.

"Yeah, I don't think that's a great idea," Levi said, putting a hand on Harper's waist. He hated when Harper and Noah had a little cocaine-laced fun. It reminded him too much of his oldest brother and the chaos that went along with it.

When Levi turned to wave at someone calling his name, Harper winked at Noah and mouthed, "Later".

When Levi turned back to Harper, she curled against him. He smelled of soap and a musky cologne. She appreciated the way she could lean into his massive frame and feel enveloped by him.

"He really shouldn't be getting so messed up when he has to go home to his kids," Levi told her as they walked toward their friends. Levi always worried about the people in their lives. He worried about his parents, his sister, the brother he never saw, all of their co-workers, and friends. Unlike a lot of other people in her life, Levi wasn't all hard edges. He had a soft side that drew her in.

"You're cute," she whispered to him before turning to greet everyone. They raised their glasses at her and shouted another round of happy birthdays.

When he slipped his arm around her waist, she reached over and planted a kiss on his smooth cheek. Harper couldn't believe she had been lucky enough to find someone like him. A few people told her it wasn't a good idea to date someone she worked with, the head piercer at Silver Sparrow Tattoos. She ignored them.

She knew things with Levi would be different. He was one of the few people in her life that understood all the things she'd been through and how they had formed her life. He didn't take advantage of her flaws and only a few times nudged her to confront them. Then again, she had done the same for him, nudging him to stand up for himself more. All those years she worried she would never find a person like Levi, but there he was.

Harper broke away from Levi the moment the first line of Push It by Salt-N-Pepa played from the jukebox. She grabbed Olive, pulling her friend to the middle of the bar to dance to their song. The two of them pushed their way into the middle of the friends to dance along to the song they had loved since they were kids.

The first time she and Olive heard Push It, they were sitting out front of their five-story walk-up. Two guys were sitting on the hood of their car in the apartment parking lot, blasting the song. It was the middle of summer and their apartments were too hot to stand. Neither of their moms had money for an air conditioner and the stagnant air inside made it worse. They were talking about how they couldn't wait to be old enough to get jobs, to get their own apartments, to make sure they could afford to stay cool when it was hot and stay warm when it was cold. Olive said they would move out, get places downtown and away from Green Bridge. Even at eleven years old, Harper doubted they would ever get out of their neighbourhood. She saw the way people in their neighbourhood lived and died there. She couldn't see why they would be any different.

Harper might not have gotten out of Green Bridge, but for the first time in her life, she had everything she needed. After her mom remarried and moved out of their neighbourhood, Harper found her own apartment, landed a solid job, and saved enough money that she could do something big with it. She might not have been wealthy, but at least she had an air conditioner.

"Shots," Noah shouted, as he maneuvered his wheelchair through the crowd with one hand, a bottle of tequila in the other, held up in the air for all to see. After filling everyone but Olive's cup, he shouted over the music, "Birthday girl, before you do your shot, tell us the one thing you're most excited for this year."

She wanted to tell them about her plans to bring in more clients for herself to Silver Sparrow Tattoos, to start saving to buy a house, and to start selling prints of her art online. Instead, she told them about her newest plan.

"This year, I plan on actually taking my vacation time and travelling around South America for a month or so." She beamed at the confession. A few of the faces were surprised, but a lot of them were happy for her. Harper had never been out of the province, let alone the country. With money in savings for the first time in her life, she wanted to see at least a little of the world.

"To getting the hell out of Green Bridge," Olive said, raising her cup of root beer. Everyone else raised their cup and shouted the same words into the bar. While she tossed her shot back, Harper noticed that one person hadn't done the same thing. Levi stood still, staring at her.

As she swallowed the warm liquid, Harper touched Levi's arm. He didn't look at her, so she moved into his line of sight and asked, "What's wrong?"

He forced a smile. His dark eyes were narrowed and wouldn't meet hers. He shook his head. "Nothing."

"Hey," Harper said, no longer being cute about it.

Levi always avoided confrontation when he could, so she held onto his wrist and reminded him, "We don't do this. We don't pretend everything's good when it's not. So, what is it?"

Before he could answer, Olive came up to them and said, "I'm gonna go. Sorry."

"What? I just got here."

Olive glanced toward the bar and Harper did too. Struggling to climb onto a bar stool near the end of the counter was Olive's mother, Angelica. Her yellow dye job stood out against the bald heads and grey hair of the men around her. Her wobbly motions and loud demands were impossible to ignore.

Any drama Harper had with her own mother paled in comparison to the things Olive went through with Angelica. Angelica was known by almost everyone in the building, often starting fights with the other tenants while intoxicated. Everyone avoided Angelica, and by extension her family, but not Harper.

"I'll get rid of her," Harper said, clenching her fists. The plastic cup in her hand crumpled.

Olive put herself between Harper and her mother. "Just leave her for now. Stay here. Focus on your party."

"Are you sure?" Harper looked at Olive and said, "I wouldn't mind a little face off with Angelica if it means you stay."

Olive shrugged. "It won't make things better. If she leaves now, she'll end up finding somewhere sketchier to go. I'm gonna go though. Sorry."

Harper took the key from her tiny black purse and said, "Stay at my place, so you don't have to deal with her when she gets home."

Olive shook her head. "It's been a bad week. I should be there when she gets back."

Levi stepped forward. "We'll walk you home."

The apartment building where Harper and Olive grew up, where Olive still lived, sat only a block away from the Swashbuckler.

Olive gave them a sympathetic smile. "I'm going to grab my stuff and say goodbye. Meet you guys outside?"

Harper turned back to Levi and said, "You going to tell me what's going on?"

"It can wait."

"No, let's talk about it now." She took his elbow and said, "Outside. Let's talk while we wait for Olive."

Levi sighed and followed her out the door.

Even though night had fallen, the temperature outside had risen, feeling more humid than during the day.

The sound of an engine coupled with the thumping of bass notes caused them to pause. Harper straightened. Levi put a hand on her waist and pushed her back into the doorway of the bar. They stood there, unmoving, as the car rolled by with its windows down. The man hanging out of the car window watched them as they passed, his skin so white it glowed in the green fluorescent light of the bar's sign.

Levi took Harper's arm and led her around the side of the Swashbuckler. The street light on that side of the bar had been broken, casting it into darkness.

Harper leaned up against the brick of the building. It wasn't enough to cool her, but it took the edge off. She noticed Levi didn't come to her, but started awkwardly pacing. He moved back and forth on the sidewalk. The sound of glass and crumbling sidewalk crunched beneath his shoes.

"What's going on?" she asked, lifting her hair to get it off her sweating neck.

Before Levi could answer, Harper's phone began to ring in her pocket. She fished into her skirt and pulled it out. The screen was bright in the lack of light outside the bar, so she had to squint to see the name. Patricia Aetos. Her mother.

Ten minutes before midnight and her mother finally remembered her birthday? Harper didn't want to hear her excuses for not calling earlier. She didn't want the night to have anything to do with her mother. Instead of accepting the call, Harper sent it to voicemail and turned her attention back to Levi.

"What's going on?" Harper asked Levi.

"You're going to travel around South America this year." He didn't ask, repeating her own statement from earlier back to her. There was tension in his jaw and in the way he moved without swinging his arms.

"Yeah," Harper said. "I'm thinking this fall. Why are you upset? Did you want to come?"

Levi stopped. "Do I want to come?"

Harper raised an eyebrow. Did he not want to be included in her travel plans? He always said he wanted to see more of the world too. It had been meeting Levi that pushed her thoughts of travel to the forefront. After he finished college, he went to Europe with his sister and Japan with his ex-girlfriend. He had already ventured out and Harper wanted to catch up.

"Do you not want to come?" Harper asked.

He looked her in the eye finally. "You could have asked me."

"I'm asking you."

He threw his hands in the air. "I mean, before you made a plan. You didn't think of including me. You made a plan without me."

Harper stood up from the wall and asked, "What is this? Am I supposed to ask your permission to travel?"

"I just wanted you to talk to me before you started making all these plans," he said. "Include me in your decisions for the future."

She could see the fight in his eyes to stay calm. Growing up in a home with his brother's addiction and rage, Levi had promised he wouldn't shout at people, even though the urge got the better of him from time to time.

Harper shook her head. "That sounds like I need to ask you permission."

Levi let out a long exhale, tamping down the urge to shout. "Harper, I'm not telling you to ask permission, but we've been together for a year and a half. We're supposed to be partners. These are things we should discuss. What if I had something in mind too and those things conflicted?"

"Did you have something in mind?" Harper asked. She figured there must have been something he'd been planning if he was getting so worked up about where she wanted to travel to.

"Yes!" he shouted. He inhaled, calming himself again, and said, "I had a thought, but I wanted to talk to you about it first. I wanted to have a discussion. As partners."

Harper rested herself against the wall again. "Well, what is it?"

Levi shook his head and resumed pacing.

Harper's phone rang again. Again, she sent it to voicemail.

"Spit it out," she told him, sighing. "Just tell me what you're thinking."

Levi grabbed his own phone from the back pocket of his jeans. He tapped aggressively on the screen. After a few swipes, he turned the screen toward her and said, "I saw this posting and I thought about asking your opinion on it."

Harper leaned in and looked at the post. The ad offered a townhouse for rent. Even before she looked at the address, she knew it wasn't in their neighbourhood. No Green Bridge house had a lawn that manicured and a road without potholes the size of ponds. They definitely didn't have wood fences that looked as new as the one in the picture.

"You're moving out of Green Bridge?"

"It's just on the other side of the bridge. It would take the same amount of time to get to Silver Sparrow every day for work, but it's a safer neighbourhood."

She handed him the phone back. "What do you need a three-bedroom townhouse for?"

"I thought we could use a three bedroom house."

The emphasis on 'we' made her stomach flip. Harper pressed herself against the rough bricks behind her. A house for her and Levi. He wanted her to move in.

"I have my own apartment," Harper told him.

Levi sighed like he'd been waiting for that conversation. "This place has a backyard. It has a full basement that you can turn into a studio or you can use one of the bedrooms."

"But I have a place." Harper had worked too hard to get an apartment that met her needs. She couldn't give up her place. What if Levi decided he didn't want to live with her anymore? What if Harper got tired after work and couldn't keep the apartment clean enough for him? What if he got bored with her or found someone he liked better? Harper couldn't end up homeless. She couldn't get tied into a lease with another person or worse, not have her name on a lease at all.

As much as Levi liked to pretend that people stayed together forever, like his parents, that everything would work out for them, Harper knew. She and her mother had lived in a car for six months after her father disappeared in the middle of the night. She watched as her mom, Patricia, struggled to find a place that would accept a twenty-two-year-old woman who had a six-year-old.

It wasn't only about the apartment. When Harper's dad left, Patricia's whole life fell to pieces. She had no money, no stability, and no time to raise her daughter. Harper made one promise to herself growing up: It didn't matter what she did or where she went, she wouldn't turn out like Patricia Aetos.

"I'm asking you to live with me, Harper," Levi told her.

Harper shook her head.

The hurt she caused flashed across his face. His mouth opened, as if he were going to speak, but then he closed it again. His eyes and nose scrunched together. When she pushed off the wall again, reaching for him, he turned away and mumbled under his breath, "Don't."

Harper wanted him to understand. Of all people, Levi should know how hard she worked to create what she had. Too many times in her life, Harper had been left with nothing. She refused to be left with nothing again.

He stopped pacing and turned to her.

He took a deep breath and said, "I'm done."

"What?"

Levi ran his hands over his head and pulled at the long strands of his thick hair. He took a second before speaking again. "I want a partner, Harper. I want someone that values my opinion and wants to discuss the future together. I want someone who can actually see us for the long haul, not someone expecting it'll fall apart."

She couldn't believe it. "You're dumping me."

He was breaking up with her. Levi was breaking up with her. On her birthday.

"Fuck. I guess I am."

Harper folded her arms across her chest. "Are you sure? Because if you break up with me now, I'm not going to take you back."

Levi's chin trembled. "I figured as much."

Harper could feel the tears stinging her eyes. She couldn't catch her breath, but she didn't want him to see that. She needed to get away before she began to sob. He didn't get to see her at her most vulnerable; He wasn't her boyfriend anymore.

Harper turned on her heel in the direction of her apartment, but before she could take a step, Levi grabbed her.

"It's not safe. Let me grab my stuff."

"I can take care of myself," she said, ripping her arm from his grasp.

Olive called to them. When Harper called back, Olive rushed around the side of the bar, her purple hair bouncing in all directions. She didn't seem to notice the tension. She thrust her phone at Harper and said, "You gotta take this. It's your mom."

Patricia had called Olive, and that didn't sit right with her. Harper wanted to push it away, but Levi and Olive stared at her.

At least, Harper thought as she took the phone, her mother remembered her birthday this year. Would this be the year she at least apologized?

"Hello?" she said into the phone, turning her back on Olive and Levi.

"Where are you?"

"Swashbuckler."

"That's disgusting," her mother spat into the phone. "I'm coming to get you."

"What? No. Why?"

"Your father, Henry. He died."

Harper knew very little about her father, but she had always figured the next time she would hear anything about the man would be when he'd died. Henry Wilde had made a point of removing himself from her and Patricia's lives without leaving a trace behind. She wasn't at all surprised by the call.

"I'll come by tomorrow and we can talk about it," Harper said, even though she wouldn't follow through. She had bigger things to deal with than the death of a stranger.

"No," her mother shouted into the phone. "It's not about Henry. It's about the kids."

"What?"

"Kids, Harper. Your dad had kids."

CHAPTER TWO

"So, remind me again why I'm here and why you thought this was a good idea," Harper said as she drove her mom's black SUV into the parking lot of the Social Services building downtown.

Multiple times, Harper told her mother to stay behind, that she didn't need the company, but Patricia wouldn't let it go. According to her, she needed to be there. Patricia was being so awkward about the whole thing that Harper agreed that they could go together, only if she was the one to drive. Patricia had a habit of getting distracted while on the road and the emotional state she was in meant it was safer with Harper behind the wheel.

"You spent your entire childhood begging me for a sibling and now that you have two, you don't want to meet them?" Patricia scoffed as she unhooked her seat belt, even though Harper hadn't finished pulling into the parking space.

Harper spent her childhood wanting a sibling because Patricia was gone all the time. As a child, Harper assumed her loneliness could only be cured by siblings, the way it had been for other people.

"I wanted to grow up with siblings, not find out about

them when I'm twenty-five," Harper told her mother as she shifted the vehicle into park.

"These are your father's children. We can't just leave them."

Harper gripped the steering wheel tighter. "Why not? Henry had no trouble leaving us behind."

It made Harper uncomfortable that her mother was the one wanting to jump in and rescue the children. Out of the two of them, Patricia seemed to grieve his departure more. Her plan to be a stay-at-home mom came to an end. She cried every day for weeks that all her plans for the future were crushed. She'd put her trust into Henry and when he left, she had to restart from scratch with a child who consumed her time and that couldn't afford to care for.

It made no sense to Harper that Patricia would want to do something for the man that crushed her so badly.

There were only two cars in the parking lot of the building. The social worker had told Patricia that they would have to be escorted to her office by security, since it was outside of standard business hours. Harper figured the two cars in the lot belonged to the security guard and the social worker.

They walked to the front steps of the beige building named Vale Social Service Centre. It seemed small compared to the skyscrapers all around it. There were luxury condos everywhere, some right next to Social Services and across from the food bank where people lined up all week long, hoping to get something to feed themselves and their families. At least in Green Bridge, Harper's neighbourhood, the majority of her neighbours were dealing with the same struggles. She didn't have rich neighbours looking down on her.

On the other side of the glass doors, the security guard stood from his desk and made his way over to let them in. Harper watched as Patricia reached out to shake the man's hand and tell him how grateful she was that he could open the doors for them that morning.

Harper had become used to Patricia's uncharacteristic displays of kindness since she moved in with the man that had become her husband. Roger came from money and had made his own money, and Patricia had started putting on a show that made people believe that she, too, came from money and hadn't lived in her car at one point in her life.

That morning, Patricia showed up wearing a cream-coloured pantsuit with a navy button-up shirt, buttoned all the way to her neck. She had fixed her hair into a tight bun and kept her make-up conservative, with only a light foundation and mascara.

Harper hadn't washed her make-up off the night before.

The security guard, a fragile looking white man in his seventies, took them to the elevator. His eyes tracked Harper's every move. It wasn't the first time Harper experienced those types of stares. Even in her own neighbourhood, her visible tattoos and the silver ring in her nose rubbed some people, often the older generation, the wrong way. They thought she was up to no good.

The elevator doors opened on a floor full of cubicles and a sign that said Family and Children's Services. Fluorescent lights illuminated everything in an intense white. They walked along one of the rows. Each space was small, with one chair behind a desk and two or three chairs on the opposite side. Most of the cubicles had desktop computers and paperwork on almost every surface.

"Beatriz?" the security guard called out from ahead of them.

A small woman with dark curls popped out from behind one of the cubicle walls. She was wearing a blue knit sweater with pink hearts and a pair of dark wash jeans. She looked like someone Olive might have one of her university classes with, not a social worker. Harper doubted the woman was even as old as she was.

It did explain her late night phone call and weekend

meeting. She had the appearance of the young, go-getter type. Her desire to do the right thing and 'be the change' hadn't been ground down by years of civil servant work. Harper had seen social workers and volunteers like her on and off throughout her life. Eventually, they stopped smiling all the time and put in the bare minimum like everyone else.

"Hi! Come in," Beatriz said, waving at them to follow her. She turned to the security guard and told him she would bring them down when their meeting ended. Harper hung back, letting Beatriz and her mother enter the cubicle first.

"I'm so sorry to drag you all the way downtown on a Saturday," Beatriz told them as she began typing on her ancient looking keyboard. At one time, it must have been white or beige, but it had yellowed with time. "If it wasn't an emergency, I would have waited until Monday."

"What's the emergency? I thought Henry Wilde died like two weeks ago," Harper said.

When Patricia had picked her up, she'd filled Harper in on the details. Henry had died while evading the police sixteen days before. He had been stealing cars for some organized crime group, according to reports. It hadn't been his first offence.

Harper asked if he had been a criminal when he and Patricia were together, but didn't get a response.

Patricia also let her know he had two children, but there was no mention of a mother in their lives. Patricia assumed their mother had been dealing with some substance abuse issues and implied that Henry might have been as well, but it seemed like speculation. Patricia had no proof. What wasn't speculation; The children were in foster care and for some reason, her mother wanted to pull them out. Despite Harper's interrogation on the drive, she hadn't been given a satisfying answer as to why.

Beatriz opened a manila folder on her desk. There were

what looked to be forms stacked on top of other forms. From where she sat, Harper couldn't see what any of them said.

"We've been trying to track you down, Miss Wilde, since your father's passing." Beatriz may have looked young, but her tone and word choices were professional, like she'd been working in the industry for decades.

Harper remembered the way the social workers spoke when she was taken into the foster system at six. At the time, she thought everyone working on her case was so old and wise. Sitting in that office years later, it occurred to her that the person handling her case could have been only in their early twenties.

"How did you track me down?" Harper asked. "And why?"

It couldn't have been Henry's idea to bring the children into her life. Once he left, he never returned. He didn't send cards or call on her birthday. He decided he didn't want to be a family man, or at least that's what Harper assumed.

Finding out he had a whole family made it harder to justify though.

"How much do you know about your father's family?" Beatriz asked.

Harper cringed at the term. "Let's just call him Henry from here on out, okay?"

"Yes, Henry. How much do you know about Henry's family? His parents."

Patricia sat up straighter. "His parents were alcoholics who routinely beat their children. Henry's brother, Harry, has been in and out of prison since he was fourteen years old."

Beatriz nodded. "He is currently incarcerated. The children's maternal grandparents are in Texas, but they have advised that they are uninterested in reunification. They do not know the whereabouts of their daughter, but she previously gave up parental rights."

They had no other family. Harper understood that. While

her mother had been working or taking night classes, no aunts or uncles, and no grandparents, stepped up to help. They were all so angry at Patricia for getting pregnant at fifteen that they wrote Harper off as well. The older Harper got and the more she heard about both sides of the family, the less she longed for that connection.

"You're aware that I haven't seen or heard from my father in almost twenty years, right?" Harper mentioned. "I don't know what you want me to do."

Beatriz sat forward. Her massive brown eyes bore right into Harper's. "We were hoping to discuss your willingness to become a guardian of Frances and Edward Wilde."

A loud laugh escaped Harper. Why would they ask her, of all people, to take on guardianship of children she had never met? She wasn't a qualified foster parent. She didn't even know how to change a dirty diaper. Other than Noah and his family, she didn't know any children.

It took her a moment to realize that Beatriz and Patricia weren't laughing, but staring at her.

"You're not joking?" Harper asked, looking between them. "You want me to take care of two kids? Like, just give up my life for two absolute strangers?"

"They are your half siblings," Patricia said, her tone scolding.

Harper wanted to ask her if she was joking. Her mother made it very clear that having a child had gotten in the way of living her life. It only made sense that Harper wouldn't make the same mistakes she had.

Harper stared at her mother. "Yeah, two kids that Henry made sure I didn't get to know. You want me to take two strangers? That's not going to happen. If Henry wanted me in their lives, he could have given me a call before he kicked it."

"Harper," her mother scolded again.

Harper expected a reaction from the social worker over her comment. She didn't get one.

Beatriz, with her composed expression, asked, "At this time, placing the eldest in a different household is our top priority."

Harper and Patricia's heads snapped in her direction.

"Just the daughter? What do you mean? Separating them?" Harper asked. "Why would you separate them?"

She might not have siblings to understand that bond, Harper couldn't imagine what would have happened to her if she and Olive hadn't found each other. They had become a pair. They were as close as siblings, and even though she'd never said it out loud, Harper couldn't imagine having made it to adulthood without her. If they had been separated, she definitely wouldn't have.

The social worker shifted in her seat. "At this time, the children are in emergency care. This is a short-term solution and these families aren't equipped to take the children in the long term. We've been able to place Edward in a long-term foster home next week."

"What about the other one? The girl?" Harper asked. It had been terrifying going into a foster home alone. No one knew her. No one understood her or where she came from. They had treated her like an outsider, because that's what she was. It had been Harper against the world with no one who knew what she'd been through. It might have been different if she had someone, anyone, to go through it with.

"The only placement we can find for Frances at this time is a group home."

Harper exhaled. Even though she'd never been old enough to end up in one, there were rumours about group homes. There were stories about bullying, abuse, and worse. She shook her head. "You have to have some other option."

Beatriz looked at Harper. "We're hoping we do."

The idea that Harper had the time or the resources to take in two children seemed far-fetched. There were too many things she needed to do. There were already plans in place for the future, like her trip. Her apartment didn't have the space for two extra bodies. Her schedule didn't have the availability. Between her social life, her job, and Levi…

In the chaos, she'd forgotten how she and Levi left things. It should have been a dream, not a nightmare. She swallowed and gave her head a shake. Getting consumed by thoughts of Levi dumping her would not help the situation.

"Keeping families together is always our first option," Beatriz said. "Our main priority."

"And we can help," Patricia said, reaching out to touch Harper's arm. "Roger and I can help."

Laughed bubbled up in Harper's throat, but she'd learned from the previous outburst to choke it down. Had her mother said that to look good in front of the social worker?

She's be on her own to take care of those kids. What would Harper do with two children? Or even one?

Leaving one of the kids in a group home, that seemed like the worst possible option. The girl wouldn't have her own room, her own space. They would take her away from her brother and leave her with nothing. Harper couldn't take on that responsibility, but why would they think that's the right thing to do to a child?

"What if Roger and I apply to foster them? Is that possible?" Patricia asked.

Harper stared at her mother in disbelief. Patricia had never wanted a child yet she wanted to take on the two children of her estranged ex-husband?

"You're serious?" Harper tilted her head, waiting for the punchline, waiting for Patricia to back peddle. "Why would you do that?"

"I'm not some monster, like you make me out to be, Harper," her mother said with a sarcastic laugh.

Harper stared at her mother.

Patricia sat up a little straighter. "You've said to me on more than a few occasions that I could have been a more involved parent. What's more involved than trying to keep you and your siblings together?"

It had to be a show Patricia was putting on for the social worker. Harper couldn't imagine her mother wanting to be more involved. It went against everything Patricia had showed her over the years. She had seemed all too happy when Harper turned down her request to live with the man she was dating.

Patricia offering to take Henry Wilde's children felt like a dig at Harper. What did Patricia want to prove? That she would have been a better mother to someone else, someone different than Harper? That's what it felt like.

Beatriz cleared her throat. "As I mentioned on the phone yesterday, you and Roger are not kin. In order to foster the children, you both would have to go through the rigorous process to receive your license to foster."

Patricia pointed at Harper. "But you'll just hand the children over to her?"

Harper raised her hands in disbelief and let them fall with a slap against her thighs.

"She would qualify for what we call a kinship placement," Beatriz said. "It's a short-term solution and if a long-term solution is needed, the kin can appeal to the court to either extend their kinship status, request full guardianship, or apply for adoption."

Patricia shook her head. "There's no way Harper can even afford to care for these children long term."

Harper raised a hand, signalling her mother to stop talking. "Hey, first of all, you don't know shit all about my finances, which are doing just fine, thank you. Secondly, you're the one that dragged me here. Why did you bother?"

"We do offer some compensation, as the children are currently in the system."

Ignoring Beatriz, Patricia gave a mocking laugh. "You live in the poorest neighbourhood in Vale."

"Are you serious right now? It's the neighbourhood you raised me in. I love Green Bridge."

"You live in what, I assume, used to be a trap house," Patricia accused.

"What are you even talking about? You knew the guy that used to live in that house. It's three apartments now and, by the way, they're really nice. You wouldn't know because you haven't even offered to come see my place since I moved in."

"Because you live in a slum."

"First of all, it's not a slum. And secondly, until you met your rich husband, you used to live there too," Harper yelled back at her. The volume of her tone pulled her out of her anger and made her aware of her surroundings again. If there had been other people in that office, if it had been a normal workday, the sound of her voice might not have been so jarring, but it echoed.

"We want to apply to foster," Patricia said.

"And you can. As I said on the phone yesterday, I have forwarded you the application you and your spouse will need to fill out. However, that process could take anywhere from four to six months to complete."

Patricia had already planned to foster the children. She'd already asked how to apply before even consulting Harper. She'd already decided Harper either couldn't or wouldn't do it.

Harper wondered what the hell her mother was up to.

"And the girl, she'd just have to stay in the group home the whole time?" Harper asked.

Beatriz nodded.

Living with Patricia had to be better than a group home, right? At least the girl would have her own room and her own things. Then there was Roger. Harper didn't know too much about her mother's new husband, but she knew how much his children loved him. He'd done something right.

Patricia leaned toward the desk, toward Beatriz. "I told you she wouldn't do it. She doesn't really have the means."

"We do plan to help with that," Beatriz said. "As the children are technically in care, even in a kinship placement until the courts determine a permanent guardianship, they're Crown wards."

"Money aside, Harper is a tattoo artist. That's not a job fit for a guardian."

Her mother thought she was incapable of taking care of children? Harper, who cooked dinners for her mom growing up and made sure her mom had clean clothes for work and dates? Her mother doubted her daughter, who had taken on multiple jobs in high school so she could pay for her own food and clothes?

She was more than capable. She might have said it out loud, if only she wasn't in such disbelief over her mother's slander.

"And the partying? Harper can't put aside drinking and going to clubs to raise two kids. I just don't—"

Harper cut her off, speaking loudly over her. "Four to six months is the standard time for my mom and Roger to get a foster licence?"

Beatriz nodded.

Six months would take them close to Christmas. With the way Patricia liked to throw around money, Harper figured they were looking at a four-month turnaround time. Things could be rushed when money was involved, she'd learned since Roger entered her mother's life.

Four months would mean pushing back her trip to tour South America. She hadn't spent any money on tickets or hotels at that point, but she had risked her relationship by even mentioning it. Didn't she have to follow through on the principle alone?

Beatriz leaned forward. "Do you want to see a picture?"

"No, thanks," Harper said.

"Yes, please," Patricia said.

Beatriz retrieved a physical photograph from the pile of papers in the folder. She held it up and beamed at them as if they were her own children. "It's a couple years old, from the first time they were in foster care, but Frances looks much the same."

"The *first* time?" Harper flinched. After her time in foster care, she spent years worrying that they were going to come back to get her. She did everything she could to make sure it didn't happen again. Even if her mother couldn't be bothered, Harper kept the apartment clean. She talked her mom out of being too proud and made her visit the food bank when the fridge was empty. Even when the hot water shut off, Harper made sure to shower in the cold every day before school, so the teachers wouldn't have a reason to report her.

Beatriz handed the photograph to Patricia.

The first thing Harper noticed was the boy, Edward. About three, with a round face and big eyes. Hazel eyes, she thought she could see in the picture, but it was hard to tell. His chubby little hand reached up and held onto his sister's.

His sister was quite a bit older than him, but had the same face, the same eyes. They were Henry's kids, no doubt about that.

In the picture, the girl, Frances, looked to be about eleven or twelve. Harper couldn't be sure. There was a scowl on her face, one that Harper recognized from her own intake picture. The hurt had manifested into anger. That stung.

At least Harper had a home to go back to. They told her that when her mother was ready, she could come back and get her. There was no chance they were going to be reunited with their family. They didn't even have the hope that their father would eventually straighten up and get custody again, the way Harper had expected from her mother.

Bile rose in her throat at the thought. She remembered all the rumours surrounding group homes, about what happened to kids in there. The bullying. The loss of autonomy. Worse things Harper didn't even allow her mind to wander to.

Patricia is better than a group home, right? Harper asked herself again. Even if she still didn't know why her mother wanted the kids so bad, the alternative made Harper uneasy. She had turned out okay despite having Patricia for a mother, and she didn't have a Roger. That was something, right?

"Four to six months," Harper said to herself.

Beatriz's eyes widened when Harper looked up at her. There was so much hope that Harper would offer to help, so many expectations in one pair of eyes.

Harper sucked back the sigh that was desperate to escape. "Alright. Let's do this."

CHAPTER THREE

"This is probably the most unhinged thing I've ever done," Harper grumbled as she pulled the last bin out of the dining room turned art studio.

Olive and Harper had spent all day preparing the apartment for the arrival of Henry Wilde's orphaned children. They packed up and shoved Harper's art supplies into any corner of the apartment they would fit, like stacked in her closet and used as a nightstand. Then they went to the thrift stores in the wealthier parts of town, which they knew to be an untapped resource. They picked up two twin-size bed frames and a single dresser. They couldn't find a second one that didn't need a lot of work to make it usable. Harper and Olive both knew that kids in foster care wouldn't be filling two dressers with their belongings.

"Don't you mean lovely?" Olive asked as she cut the plastic on one of the two mattresses in a box they bought that morning. "What you're doing is lovely!"

The mattress sprang out of Olive's grip and knocked a bottle of water and a cellphone off the coffee table.

Harper abandoned the last plastic bin in the hallway in order to help with the mattress. "No, I mean unhinged. Like, why did I think it was a good idea to take on two grieving kids, who are strangers, despite what the social worker says. Dude, I live in a one-bedroom apartment."

"It's a one bedroom plus a den. That's what the ad said," Harper told her with a laugh. She took one side of the mattress and Harper took the other. They carried it through the double pocket doors and tossed it onto one of the beds.

They both stood back and looked at what they'd put together. The room was the brightest in the apartment, and Harper hated to give it up. Since they couldn't move the oak desk Harper thrifted when she first moved into the apartment, it remained in the bow window. They placed the beds up against the walls on either side. There was no semblance of privacy, but it wouldn't be forever.

Four to six months, Harper reminded herself. But then what, they stayed with her mom? For how long? And honestly, why? It didn't bode well for her.

"You're doing a really awesome thing and maybe you'll really end up enjoying having the kids here," Olive said as she wiped her forehead with the back of her hand. Despite the window air conditioning running since they woke up that morning, the apartment had grown hot as the day went on.

"It's adorable that you think that. But realistically, this is going to be a nightmare." Harper glanced out of the room and into the kitchen, checking the clock on the microwave. Almost four-thirty. The kids would be there any minute. "I guess we better get the beds made."

Harper stepped back into the living room to grab the sheets and picked her phone up from the ground. There were several text messages. Her heart ached at the thought one of them might be from Levi. He hadn't responded to her last message asking if they could talk. His previous response to talking had been 'not now'.

The messages weren't from Levi, but Patricia. She wanted to know when the kids were coming, if Harper needed money to buy them food or toiletries. Twice she offered to come over to the house, despite previously refusing to return to Green Bridge for anything. She would come for children she'd never met, but not her own daughter.

Harper typed out a quick message.

> Kids coming today. I've got it under control.

"Hey," Olive said, coming up behind her. "I'm going to get out of here so you can have some time alone with the kids."

"That's the opposite of what I want." Harper sighed as she shoved the phone in her pocket. "But I'll come outside with you and wait."

With a hug and some words of encouragement, Olive left. Harper sat on the cool concrete step, waiting. The sun was too hot and she could smell the garbage in the bins only a few feet from the porch.

A blue van with patches of rust around the wheel wells and door handles came to a stop in front of the walkway. Harper's shoulders tensed and she got to her feet.

A group of pre-teens who had been playing soccer in the street stopped to watch when Beatriz got out of the vehicle. They knew she was a social worker. Like Harper had at their age, they learned to watch out for anyone who could take them away or get them in trouble. Recognizing cops and social workers was a life skill necessary in that neighbourhood.

Beatriz came around to the passenger side of the van with a wave before pulling the sliding door open. Harper held her breath.

From inside the van, Beatriz scooped up a boy with ash brown hair from the car seat. From what they'd told Harper, he turned five in March, but he seemed small for his age. When Beatriz set him down on the curb, he stood where she placed him. His eyes never left her, never wandered to the area around them. He didn't look at Harper. The pre-teen boys from the street had stepped up on the sidewalk to inspect the new arrivals, and the young boy hadn't noticed.

Edward, Harper reminded herself. Henry's son was Edward. His daughter, Frances. She had made notes while in the Social Services office.

Frances climbed out of the van and Harper could feel the panic flooding through her body, starting in her chest. The girl wasn't a child like in the picture the social worker had. Frances Wilde was a lanky teenager. A teenager, a hormonal teenager.

The girl had a hardened scowl on her face and her arms were folded against her chest. She wasn't short for her age, the way her brother was. If anything, she was tall. Not as tall as Harper was at fifteen, but likely had some height on the majority of girls in her grade.

Both children had round faces with soft edges to their jaw and hazel eyes. They had their father's narrow nose and his full lips. Harper could definitely see Henry Wilde in them, at least the details of him that she remembered.

"Let's go meet Harper and see where you'll be staying," Beatriz said as she handed backpacks to both of Henry's kids. The little boy tried to reach for Beatriz's hand, but she reached back into the van to grab a pair of black duffle bags. Harper winced at the situation.

The three of them came up the uneven walkway toward the house. The girl, Frances, kept her scowl perfectly intact and made eye contact long enough to let Harper know she was not happy about the situation.

The little boy, on the other hand, stared up at her with his wide eyes. His blue backpack, which was bigger than his torso, bounced against his back when he moved.

"Hey Harper," Kenny, one of the pre-teens who were playing soccer, shouted from the sidewalk. He was friends with Olive's younger sister and he'd often been at their apartment when Harper was.

Beatriz and the kids turned to look at Kenny.

"Who is crazy enough to let you take care of kids?" Kenny shouted at her. Beatriz and the kids stared at him. He kept a straight face until Harper rolled her eyes. At her reaction, he let out a high-pitched laugh and ran off.

"Sorry," Harper said with a sigh. "He's friends with my best friend's sister."

When Harper looked at the kids again, she caught Frances scanning her up and down. People did it all the time to her, especially when she left Green Bridge. When she needed things that the local grocery store didn't carry, she endured glares that focused mostly on her piercings, tattoos, and ripped jeans.

Harper had specifically worn non-ripped jeans for the occasion and a long-sleeve shirt despite the heat, to hide the tattoos on her arms, but it didn't stop the look of disdain.

"Frances. Edward, better known as Eddie. This is Harper."

The little boy, Eddie, glanced up at Harper and asked, "Why do you have bars on the window?"

"Because people clearly get robbed and murdered in this neighbourhood," Frances said.

"Crime happens everywhere." Harper reached out to take a bag from Beatriz. "Why don't we go inside?"

"Yeah–" Frances muttered, "–so we don't get shot."

They walked into the foyer, where the stairs took the other two tenants up and down the stairs to their apartments. Next to the stairs, only a foot from Harper's door, was a closet. "Coats and extra shoes can go in here. Boots in the winter stay out here and not in the apartment."

No one said anything, so she pushed open the front door to her apartment and let them in. After the short hallway, she gestured to the main room.

"This is the kitchen and living room. We don't have an

official dining room, but that opens up," Harper said, gesturing to the table that they passed on their way in. Harper then pointed to the rooms on either side of the main space. "Your bedroom is that way. My room and the bathroom are on the opposite side of the living room."

The kids stood behind the grey sectional that made up the main seating in the living room. Their eyes searched every inch of the apartment and for the first time Harper thought about the place the way they or the social worker might see it.

Harper didn't have a lot of things, but she liked it that way. She had only the basic furniture. No extra bedding in the cupboards or towels for guests. The only pillow on her couch had been given to her by Silver Sparrow Tattoos when they ordered too many for the shop couches. The lamp by the television didn't match the one on the end tables. Harper suddenly became aware of the line drawings of naked people that she had behind the television. She only noticed them because the little boy let out a giggle when his eyes landed them.

"I'll have to take those down for the time being," Harper said to the social worker.

Beatriz laughed, but said nothing. She handed over a folder with paperwork she would need to get them enrolled in school in September and pamphlets on what programs the children could sign up for. She said that there were no allergies to worry about and no medical conditions that they were aware of.

While she listened, Harper watched the children. They stared back at her like caged animals watching their captor. Checking for weaknesses that they could use to escape later. Frances' death stare grew deeper the longer Harper stayed focused on them, but she couldn't tear her eyes away.

Those children were the ones that Henry Wilde decided to stay with. Those were the children he deemed worthy of his time. Frances had fourteen years with her father. By the time Harper was six, he'd cut off all contact. She couldn't even be sure if Henry knew she was still in the city.

"You can take a look at your room or the bathroom," Harper said, hoping the kids and Beatriz would give her some physical distance so she could process.

They didn't move.

Harper could feel the awkwardness and tension rising in the space. She knew she had to say something. She needed to acknowledge the kids but she had no idea how.

"So," Harper said, looking between both of the children. "I'm really sorry to hear about your dad. I can't even–"

The girl cut her off. "I don't want to talk about him with you."

Harper could handle a little attitude. "I didn't know him, but clearly he loved you and I'm sure–"

"Ugh." Frances cut her off again. "You don't get to talk about our dad. He didn't want you. I don't either."

Harper froze.

Beatriz put her hand on Frances' shoulder and said, "You might be hurting, but that doesn't give you the right to hurt other people."

She didn't expect to be shut down so hard when offering condolences. She definitely didn't plan on being roasted by a fourteen-year-old in the process.

The boy didn't seem at all concerned by his sister's words. He reached for her and said, "We get to share a room."

"Oh goody," Frances replied, her words dripping with sarcasm.

Beatriz gave an encouraging smile. "Remember, this is a temporary situation."

The fact that they knew and that they understood it was temporary was a relief. Harper didn't know how she would have a conversation like that. She had been trying to figure out how to word it without sounding like she couldn't wait to get rid of them.

"But it seems like everything else is in order," Beatriz said as she closed her bag.

She told the children if they wanted to get in touch with her, they only had to ask Harper. Beatriz asked Harper to walk her out. Nodding at Beatriz, and after letting the kids know she would be right back, Harper followed the social worker outside.

"Well, thank you for doing this," Beatriz said when they made it out to the porch.

Harper nodded. Not sure what else to say.

"I'll call to check in from time to time. Fill out those direct deposit forms I sent you though, okay? As I mentioned in our first meeting, there is compensation for kinship care, so this way we can get the money to you faster than a cheque in the mail."

Harper hated the idea of the government funding her life, like she couldn't handle things on her own. Her mother would have scoffed at getting payments like that. She would too.

"I don't know if that's necessary."

Harper crossed her arms and then uncrossed them.

Beatriz put a hand on Harper's wrist. "Think about this money as theirs. It's for them. They need it."

Their money, Harper reminded herself.

"Thanks. I'll make sure I put it to good use," Harper said. Harper refused to keep the money for herself like the family who had fostered her. Despite not having shoes that fit or any proper boots for winter, Harper returned to her mother in the same things she left in.

"I can see you're overwhelmed," Beatriz said.

Harper snorted a laugh. "I thought I was keeping my shit together."

Beatriz shook her head. She no longer seemed younger

than Harper. Clearly she knew how to handle situations like the one she was in far better than Harper ever would. It gave her an air of authority. "Remember, no one will force you to remain the carer for Frances and Edward, but what you're doing now is really great. You're keeping siblings together and I can't express how much I appreciate it."

Harper met the social worker's gaze. She had to wonder if it was some ploy to ease her into the situation and then ask her to keep the kids.

"Remember to reach out if you need anything. Outside of financial support, we have connections to resources that can help, like summer camps, therapy, things like that," Beatriz told her. "There are some details in the folder I left with you."

"I will look into it when they go to bed tonight," Harper told her, even though all she wanted to do was stretch out, watch a movie, and pop a THC gummy or two.

It felt like the end of the conversation, but Beatriz didn't move. She switched her bag from one hand to the other before saying, "This is a really big change for all of you. You were strangers, but even if this arrangement turns out to be very short term, it could be a really good chance for you to get to know your family."

Harper had people she was related to by DNA, and time and again they let her down. Her grandparents kicked her mom out when she was pregnant, instead of helping their teen daughter. Henry bailed for greener pastures the minute things got difficult. Patricia had stuck around, but only in the most basic sense. It didn't seem like more family would change the situation.

"Thanks," Harper said, because she didn't know what else would be right in a moment such as that.

Beatriz nodded before turning and walking to her van. Harper watched as she pulled away from the curb, forced to deal with the kids playing soccer, who patted her car loudly as she inched past them.

Harper knew she had to go back inside and face the kids. Logic said she had to make an effort while they were living under her roof, but she didn't want to. Every muscle in her body ached to run, to head down to the Swashbuckler for a beer, or find Levi and convince him not to leave her.

The walk back into the house felt both too short and very long. She closed the door to the house, and when inside the apartment, closed that door too. After kicking off her shoes, she took in the two faces staring at her.

"So," Harper said. "It's basically dinnertime. What do you guys like to eat? I can order whatever."

"No," Frances said, not looking up from her hands. "We're going to go to bed."

"Are you sure? I can order anything. It doesn't matter."

Frances rolled her eyes.

Eddie climbed onto the couch and asked. "Can we have pizza?"

Before Harper could answer, Frances said, "No. I packed us sandwiches. We're going to eat those and go to bed."

Harper checked the window to make sure she wasn't losing it. "Go to bed? It's only like five o'clock. Honestly, I can order pizza."

Frances grabbed her backpack from where she left it on the floor and shouted, "We're forced to stay. But I don't want a single thing from you. Not your food and not your pity."

Harper straightened her shoulders and tipped her chin. "Alright. That's fair. You do your thing, and if you decide to calm the hell down, there will be pizza on the counter in the next thirty-ish minutes."

"Don't count on it." Frances stormed into their temporary bedroom and turned her attention to her brother. "Eddie, come eat your sandwich."

Harper expected some rebellion from the boy. Maybe a pout or a groan, but he got up from the couch and walked into the space that had once been Harper's studio. She wished she could be in there with her desk and her music blasting, just sketching and not thinking about anything at all.

The pocket doors slammed shut in her face.

Harper clenched her fists. She wanted to scream as loud as she could, but she knew it would give the girl the upper hand.

In the span of two days she'd lost her boyfriend and had her birthday cut short. Doors slamming in her face seemed like the cherry on top of the already horrible sundae. To deal, she couldn't curl up in bed and ignore the world. She also couldn't go out and drink or get high with her friends.

Instead, she threw herself onto the couch and ordered pizza. Too much pizza, which she ended up eating alone.

CHAPTER FOUR

BEING BORN AND RAISED IN GREEN BRIDGE, HARPER FORGOT how the neighbourhood could appear to people not from the area. The kids stayed close to each other as they followed her along the sidewalk. Frances even muttered 'gross' under her breath when they passed the abandoned house halfway to the shop.

It surprised her. From what she knew about Henry Wilde's life after he left, he'd been a criminal and on the run from the police at least once. Had their lives really been that different from hers?

"You didn't live in a neighbourhood like this?" Harper asked. She had to slow her speed several times so Eddie could keep up.

"Our building had a pool," Eddie said, his chest puffed up. "But it was broken sometimes."

"It was still a lot nicer than here," Frances told her.

Harper bit her tongue. As much as she wanted to defend Green Bridge, she knew that it wasn't the time. Frances and Eddie had been through a lot. They didn't need to get scolded, at least that's what the internet told her when she searched for how to deal with grieving kids. The websites and forums told her to 'give them grace'.

One thing she appreciated about the kids, she didn't even have to ask them to get ready. By the time she woke up that morning, both of them were sitting in their room, fully dressed. The empty pizza boxes meant they ate, even though there were no signs of dishes laying around. Frances looked relieved when Harper said they had to get out of the apartment for a couple hours.

At least until she got out into the neighbourhood.

The block Silver Sparrow Tattoos sat on had become less rundown than the rest of the neighbourhood. The owners, Maz and Noah, helped their neighbours fix up their businesses. Having two well-known artists at the tattoo shop brought people into the area who might otherwise avoid Green Bridge. The only one bringing in more business was the Indian restaurant across the street that had an award-winning biryani.

Harper stopped in front of the shop and dug into her bag for her keys.

"We're going in there?" Frances asked, staring at the massive silver sparrow on the window, not hiding her disgust. "I don't think kids are allowed in a tattoo place."

Harper looked at her as she retrieved the keys and said, "I work here. I have one scheduled appointment and then we'll get some groceries."

"So, we have to sit around here while you work?" Frances spit the words out.

Harper didn't bother to answer, but used that moment to take several deep breaths to reduce her heart rate. She didn't expect Frances to be grateful for Harper taking them in, but couldn't she at least cut the attitude?

In the shop, music played from somewhere in the building. Black metal. It meant that Maz had been the first to arrive.

Maz, who co-owned the shop with Noah, decided who got control of the music for the first half of the day based on who showed up and started working first. Incentive to get into the shop and get the behind-the-scenes stuff started. If it had been some experimental indie artist or upbeat hip-hop, Harper would have known Noah made it in before anyone else.

Once the kids were inside, Harper locked the door behind them, and said, "This is Silver Sparrow Tattoos."

The inside of the shop looked like it belonged in a more upscale neighbourhood of Vale, not in Green Bridge. The floors were a metallic silver epoxy which contrasted with the black walls, but paired well with the exposed metal beams and ventilation above. To add some less industrial elements, the front desk had a wood countertop, and the backdrop separating the waiting room from the rest of the building, was covered in plants. As an apprentice, Harper had spent a lot of time watering the living wall and pruning any dead leaves from the plants.

"This way," Harper said, waving them to follow. She smiled to herself when she heard Eddie whisper, "So cool."

Behind the living wall, the building stretched out long and narrow, like all of the buildings on that block. There were three workstations on either side, making room for the six artists to work. The stations had half walls, giving enough privacy, but keeping everything open. The back of the shop was enclosed and housed four doors: bathroom, storage, break room, and office.

Harper led the kids into the break room. "You've gotta hang out here," she said, tossing her bag onto the massive leather sectional.

Unlike the rest of the building, the walls in the break room were grey. The lighting wasn't as bright. Computers and printers sat next to a set of lockers no one ever used. By the time everyone showed up, there would be things scattered everywhere, on every surface in that room. The small kitchenette on the opposite wall had a full-size refrigerator, a toaster oven, and a sink which would be covered in takeout.

"The bathroom is right across the hallway. And you can go out back down that hallway, but you don't leave the patio out there. Don't go down the alleyway. And don't touch these computers," Harper said. She pointed to the television across from the sectional. "This gets every streaming service you can think of, so that should keep you busy. I just have one client. I won't take walk-ins today."

"You can't just dump us here," Frances responded. She stood with her bony hands on her hips, glaring at Harper.

"The girl's got a point." Noah rolled his wheelchair into the break room. His baby blue eyes moved from Harper's face to the children. He widened them every time they landed back on her.

After sizing up the situation, he gave the kids a wave and then turned his attention back to Harper. "I heard what's going on. Reschedule your clients for today."

Harper shook her head. "It's just one client."

The muscles in his jaw flexed. She could feel his frustration.

Noah glanced past Harper to the kids and said, "Hang out here for just a second. We'll be right back." When he looked at Harper again, he told her, "Office. Now."

Harper slunk behind Noah out of the break room and to the next door to the left. Her stomach twisted as she did. She didn't want to get scolded by Noah or Maz. She hated when they tried to parent her because they were over a decade older than she was.

Noah pushed the door to the office open and maneuvered his way inside.

Maz sat behind her desk, typing away on her laptop.

Silver Sparrow Tattoos had been Noah's idea. He wanted a shop that everyone felt comfortable in. Being a full-time wheelchair user, he bounced from shop to shop looking for one that supported him as an artist. He saw all the things that worked and that didn't, and decided he would create a place that met other people's needs as well as his own. Hating the idea of dealing with the business side of things, he recruited business major and his soon-to-be sister-in-law, Maz.

When Maz noticed Harper, she shut her laptop and asked, "What the hell are you doing here? Olive came by and told us all about what happened. I thought you would have rescheduled."

Her deep brown eyes locked on Harper. Confusion caused her to purse her lips.

"I'm sorry about your dad, dude," Maz said.

"Hey, you don't even have to worry about that. I didn't know him."

While Maz and Noah were in their early mid-thirties, no one would have guessed Maz was. She had youthful dark skin and the style of a rebellious sixteen-year-old with baggy jeans and way too many bracelets on her arms.

Noah cleared his throat. He was still annoyed that Harper had brought the kids to the shop, but he was holding back while Maz gave sympathies for the both of them.

"I have to keep my clients. I need the money," she told them. "Especially right now."

Maz and Noah exchanged glances. Harper hated how they could communicate without saying a single thing. Any other time, she also appreciated it, since it made them a great team.

Noah leaned on the edge of his desk and asked, "You know Levi isn't here, right?"

The muscles between her shoulder blades tightened. "No. I didn't even think about Levi."

It was a lie. She'd spend the night thinking about things to text him, things that might get him to text her back.

Maz cleared her throat. "He took some vacation time. He's taking the week to go visit his parents."

As much as Levi loved his family, his family stressed him out. His parents always leaned on his for emotional support and it wore him down. That, she realized, he deemed better than seeing her. That stung. Harper had been telling him for years to tell him parents he couldn't always be their sounding board, that he couldn't fix everything in their family. He never would. He didn't want to be combative, like his brother had been.

Noah turned to Maz and said, "She brought the fucking kids here."

Harper hoped the music outside of the office drowned out the sound of his voice.

Maz let out a long sigh. "Dude, you know you can't. Noah owns the place and he doesn't even bring his kids when we're open."

Harper didn't want to admit that she forgot about work and about her client once she got the call about Henry Wilde. Having the kids in the shop might be frowned upon, but she didn't want to seem unprofessional by canceling the appointment at the last minute.

"It's one client and we'll be out of here," she reminded them.

"You need to find a babysitter," Noah told her.

"I'll figure something out."

Maz nodded.

Noah cleared his throat. "You can't pull this shit here. When you take on the responsibility of children, you have to put all your shit aside."

He said it as if she didn't know that. The statement annoyed her and she folded her arms, biting the inside of her cheek to keep from starting an argument.

"If you need to modify your hours, we can figure that out," Maz told her.

Harper shook her head. "No way. I need to build my clientele. I can't be cutting my hours. Plus, I have bills to pay. There's gonna be three of us eating off my pay cheques for the next couple months."

Noah looked her in the eye. "We'll give you one dead-dad pass, but you pull this garbage again and you'll be finding a new shop." Noah didn't bluff.

Harper held up a hand like an oath. "I promise. I'll get a sitter." How she'd pull that off, she had no clue.

Maz and Noah turned to each other. Maz tipped her chin and Noah rolled his wheelchair back. From behind his desk, he grabbed a large brown bag with black tissue paper coming out of the top.

"What's that?" Harper asked.

Maz smiled. "For the kids."

"Come on," Noah said. "Let's give it to them."

Harper let them leave the office first so she could exhale and release the tension in her shoulders. The three of them went into the break room where Frances and Eddie were searching for something to watch on the massive flat-screen. Frances pretended not to hear them come in, but Harper could see her posture straighten.

Eddie, on the other hand, climbed off the seat and pointed to the bag in Noah's hand. "What is that?"

Frances turned too.

Harper introduced Maz and Noah to the kids. Eddie looked excited to talk to more adults. Frances didn't meet anyone's eyes.

"We got you guys some stuff to welcome you to the Silver Sparrow family," Maz told them, gesturing to Noah to hand the bag over. Eddie snatched it and ran back to the couch.

Harper wrapped her arms around herself. They all watched as Frances took the black tissue paper and folded it in perfect squares, placing it on the couch next to her. Eddie pulled out the Silver Sparrow t-shirts. They were black long-sleeved shirts with the name of the shop on the front in silver and a silver sparrow outline on the left arm. The gift bag also included branded sweaters in the same style, tote bags, and stickers. Eddie grabbed an envelope from the bag and held it up.

"What's this?"

Noah rolled over and said, "You give that to your sister to hold on to. There are some gift cards in there for you two to spend on whatever you want."

Eddie handed it to Frances.

Harper looked at Maz, eyes wide. "You didn't have to do that."

"Why not?" Maz asked. "The whole team pitched in. We wanted to."

"Because I can handle it," Harper told her.

Maz clapped a hand on her shoulder, shaking her head with a look of amusement on her face. "Yeah, we know. But why not just accept things when they're offered to you?"

Harper hated the unease that filled her. The same feeling took over when Levi mentioned things like moving in together, planning trips together, the future. She hated it.

"I gotta go print off some stencils and set up my station," Harper said, stepping away from the situation. As she walked out of the room, she could hear Maz sigh.

CHAPTER FIVE

"Don't pick your nose," Harper said, reaching out to swat Eddie's hand away from his face. "That's disgusting."

A woman who had been standing in line behind them at the coffee kiosk had been watching them the entire time. When Harper stood back up, satisfied that Eddie wouldn't shove his finger up his nose again, she noticed the woman in a knit sweater and dress pants glaring at her.

Harper glared back. "Can I help you with something?"

The woman gave a snort of disgust and turned toward the barista.

"Here," Olive said, handing Harper her cup before passing the kids theirs. Eddie shouted his thank you before immediately sucking all the whipped cream off the top of his hot chocolate. When Harper offered him a lid, he turned his whole body away as a rejection. Frances acted as if the latte had been forced on her; She wrinkled her nose up at it as she walked away from the counter. By the way Olive cleared her throat and asked where they were going next, Harper knew she wasn't supposed to acknowledge Frances' rudeness.

"Can we look at puppies?" Eddie asked. Whipped cream clung to his nose and chin.

"There's no pet store here," Harper told them. "And we don't do pet stores anyway. Puppy mills."

"But," Olive said, redirecting the conversation in her upbeat voice, "You have a Build-A-Bear gift card. Maybe you can get a stuffed dog."

Eddie's eyes widened. He nodded hard.

"Is there anywhere you want to go?" Olive asked Frances. "I know you didn't get to bring a lot of clothes with you. Do you want to use one of your gift cards to get some clothes?"

"No."

Harper's phone vibrated. Hoping Levi was responding to her texts, she grabbed it from her bag. It was just a message from her mother.

> Just so you know, I'm coming by your place tomorrow and I'm bringing my old phone for Frances, then I'll take them clothes shopping.

Harper typed out a quick response.

> No need. Handled.

"How about a phone?" Harper offered Frances. Eddie waved at them to follow him toward the Build-A-Bear store and they did.

Frances didn't look at her. "No."

Harper wondered how long she had to keep playing nice if the girl was going to shut down every opportunity to create some peace. She needed to get Frances a phone and both of them some clothes or else her mom would think she couldn't handle it. Harper didn't need her help.

Olive kept up her perky attitude. "Don't you want to text your friends? I'm sure they're missing you."

Eddie stopped walking, some hot chocolate spilling over

his fingers. "Frances doesn't have any friends. They think she's weird."

Harper cringed as if it were said about her. Teachers and other adults always talked about how she was so mature, how she was an old soul. It seemed like a compliment, like she had done something right. By the time she was sixteen, it sounded more like a comment on how she was raised than anything she'd done right or wrong.

"Shut up," Frances hissed at her brother. She kept walking and Eddie rushed to follow her. Some of his hot chocolate sloshed onto the mall floor. Neither Harper nor Olive rushed to follow them.

"Uh oh," Olive whispered as she pulled a napkin from her pocket and wiped up the spilled hot chocolate. "Is she going to end up a social outcast like us?"

"We were hardly social outcasts," Harper said, shaking her head in disbelief.

Olive and Harper had lots of friends, but they weren't classmates. They had friends who lived on their block, in their building. They always had places to go on weekends and they never missed a party. Sure, in school they struggled socially, but they had friends who had the same interests, friends whose families also struggled with things like money, addiction, and stability. She couldn't see why Olive always dunked on those relationships, even if they had all gone different ways in life. She knew Olive wanted to get out of Green Bridge, but did she have to leave all those people behind?

When enough distance was between them and the children, Olive said, "I wonder if things were already hard with them before their dad died."

Harper sipped her black coffee before saying, "Well, they were in foster care before this, their mother abandoned them, and their father died running away from the cops. So, I would say that your hunch is probably right."

Olive grabbed Harper's arm. "All of that? For real?"

Harper nodded. "I tried to talk to them about it and Frances is having none of it. She told me to shut up last night when I asked if they had any pictures of their dad they wanted to put up."

Olive let out a quiet whimper. "Those poor kids. How do you even process something like that?"

"Repress it all like the rest of us?" Harper said with a shrug and a chuckle.

"God, I hope not," Olive said, putting a hand to her chest in a display of sadness.

Harper wondered what Olive would do to make the kids talk. She grew up in a family of four kids. While her older brother had been gone for about a year, Olive knew how to get through to her siblings. They looked up to her, trusted her. Harper would settle for Frances not glaring at her.

"So, what did you want to ask me?" Olive asked as they walked into the store. "You invited me here to ask something, didn't you?"

The lights in the store were even brighter than in the mall itself. All the colours were blues and reds and yellows. She didn't know if she'd ever stepped foot in a store for kids before. Maybe, she thought, when she was too young to remember it.

Harper picked up a white stuffed bear covered in little pink hearts and gave it a squeeze. The only stuffed animals she had came from friends at birthday parties. Birthday parties stopped a year after Henry left her mom and so did the stuffed animals. Her mother spent a whole year in bed before they were evicted. The parties stopped until Harper was old enough to plan her own.

"I wanted to ask what jobs you're working during the days right now. Kabir's Kitchen is still at night, right?"

Olive wiggled one hand flat in front of her as if saying so-so. "During the day, nothing unless I can pick up a shift at the gas station. Still working overnights there. Kabir's is Saturday to Tuesday now, but if his nephew goes back to school in the fall, I'll get more hours."

With that many hours under her belt, Harper knew she couldn't ask Olive to take time out of her schedule to watch Frances and Eddie. While hiding out in the Silver Sparrow bathroom, before Olive showed up to go with them to the mall, Harper had done a quick internet search to find out if she could leave a five-year-old alone with a fourteen-year-old. While not illegal, it was not advisable for extended periods of time, according to a Reddit post.

"What is it?" Olive asked.

"I just need a sitter. I don't know what to do with the kids and I don't know how safe it would be to leave them with someone else," Harper admitted. "Does anyone in your building babysit anymore since Dora left to live with her son? Like, it's a paid gig."

"I can do it. Bella and Bryson are staying at my aunt's until school's back on," Olive said. "Kabir doesn't need me on Tuesdays and tips are the worst that day. I just can't do weekends."

"I need someone Saturday too though. I can pay double."

Harper realized Olive had kept her eyes on the kids the entire time. She set down the stuffed animal to do the same thing.

"You don't have to pay me."

Harper stared at her in surprise. "Did you think I wasn't going to pay you?"

"You don't have the money."

Had Harper's mother been talking to Olive about her finances too? "I have money. What are you talking about? For the first time in my life, I can pay all my bills and still enjoy myself. Guess what, I even have a savings account."

"But that's money for your trip."

"I can't believe you thought I wasn't going to pay you."

"Well, I'll take the job, but you still need to find someone for Saturdays. Tips on Saturdays are too good to pass up," Olive told her.

Eddie came running over and said, "Look at this." His hot chocolate-covered fingers gripped the empty body of a dalmatian.

"Where's your hot chocolate?" Harper asked, glancing around. She didn't see a spill, but she couldn't imagine he'd finished it already.

"I want this one," Eddie said, waving the animal up toward them. "Can I get it?"

"Hopefully that's the only one you touched," Olive said with a laugh as she took it from his hands to look at it.

"Eddie," Harper said, more sharply. "Where is your drink?"

Frances appeared from behind a rack, Eddie's hot chocolate-stained cup in one hand and her own in the other. Harper sighed with relief.

"Can I get this one?" Eddie asked again.

Olive tucked the dog under one arm, pulled a set of sanitizing wipes from her bag and started to clean his hands. "Of all the stuffed animals in here, are you sure that's the one that you want?"

While Harper watched Olive cleaning him up, she thought about what she would do for Saturdays. She couldn't leave Frances to watch her little brother, especially since they usually went for drinks after work.

Even if she wanted to cut back her hours, Saturday would be the worst day to pick. Most of her clients fought for those Saturday appointments. Being a young artist in the business, she didn't have the privilege to keep obscure hours.

"Why don't you go tell that lady at the counter that you want to take this one and she will help you get him all customized for you," Olive said, turning him toward the counter. Frances and Eddie headed to the employee.

"I have an idea for Saturdays," Olive said as they ambled over to the counter.

"You can't take the time off work, even if I pay you," Harper told her. "I can't pay you enough."

Olive shook her head. "Not me. Your mom. Patricia wants the kids anyway. She can watch them on Saturdays."

"I am not asking Patricia."

Olive shrugged. "I don't know what other option you have."

CHAPTER SIX

As the taxi pulled into the White Oaks neighbourhood, Frances and Eddie bickered about what show they wanted to watch later for the first half of the drive, but it faded the closer they got to Patricia and Roger's. They sat up straighter and stared out at the increasingly large houses as they passed.

The taxi stopped in front of a driveway. The gates were open, but from the road the shrubbery hid the house. Eddie let out an audible gasp. Harper chuckled, because she'd felt the same way the night Patricia dragged her to meet Roger for the first time. All Harper could think was 'We don't belong here'. She learned that Patricia definitely did. She'd been working toward that life for herself all those years.

Harper thanked the driver and they all climbed out of the car. No one spoke as they headed up the cobblestone toward the house.

For that neighbourhood, Roger's place might be called modest. Instead of adding an attachment onto the house, like the real estate agent had suggested when he bought the place, he opted to keep the green space and filled it with trees and a massive pond out back. Most of the houses in the area were almost twice the square footage and of modern design.

Roger and his late wife kept the Tudor style. As overwhelming as the massive house felt to Harper, she found the arched doorway and abundance of greenery in the landscaping to be charming. She never planned on saying that out loud though.

"It's so big," Eddie said.

Frances' head bobbed in agreement, before she turned to Harper and said, "If your mom is rich, why do you live where you live? I think I heard gunshots the other night."

Harper couldn't argue with the gunshots. There was a chance, but there was also a chance she'd mistaken the backfiring of a car from down the street. Harper tried not to let out an annoyed sigh. "This is my mom's husband's house. He has the money."

"She can't give you money?" Eddie asked.

"I don't need her money. My mom wanted to come start a new family here with Roger and his boys, so that's what they did. And, honestly, my family is back in Green Bridge with Olive, Maz, and Le... Noah."

The door to the house opened and Patricia came out with her arms spread out wide like she was auditioning for a soap opera or some stage production. Roger poked his head out from the door and gave a wave.

Patricia couldn't help herself. She rushed across the driveway, her cotton pants flowing in the breeze as she swooped in and hugged both of the children without asking. Harper didn't even get a reaction from her mother when she told Patricia to give the kids some space. Eddie hugged her back, but Frances bristled.

"Hi, welcome. Look at you beautiful children. So much like your father." She gave a dramatic sigh. "I'm so sorry to hear about your dad. You must be so heartbroken."

"I miss my daddy," Eddie said and his little chin quivered.

Harper reached out to give his shoulder a squeeze or

maybe his head a pat, but Patricia pulled him into another hug and said, "Of course you do, sweetheart."

Harper furrowed her eyebrows at the over-the-top display. Who was her mother trying to impress? It had to be Roger. Patricia had never been affectionate toward Harper, at least not in a long time. She couldn't even remember the last time her mother attempted to hug Harper.

The thought stung.

Hoping to end the situation, Harper suggested, "Let's go inside and get out of the heat." While it wasn't even the hottest day that week, she wanted Roger to intervene. He always had a way of keeping her mom a little less frustrating than normal.

Her mother acted as if she hadn't heard a single word. "I'm Patricia. Did Harper tell you about me?"

"She said you moved here to start a new family without her," Eddie said so matter-of-factly that Harper burst out laughing. She appreciated the unbridled honesty from someone so small.

Patricia glared at Harper, who shrugged.

"Let's meet everyone else," Patricia said, trying to regain control of the situation.

Roger and his boys were waiting in the hallway when they all stepped inside the house. Patricia rushed to his side, looped her arm through his, and said, "Frances, Eddie, this is Roger and his sons Kayden and Elijah."

Frances and Eddie paid no attention to the three additional strangers in front of them. Their eyes scanned every corner of the house they could see from the centre of the foyer. Frances craned her neck to get a look into the sitting room, as they called it, that Roger and Patricia only used when guests visited. Harper wondered if they saw the place the way she did. It didn't take knowing anything about fabrics and luxury materials to know that she couldn't afford even the grey drapes in that living room.

"Hi," Roger's boys said in unison, trying to get Frances' and Eddie's attention. Harper tapped the kids' shoulders and nodded at them to pay attention to the people standing in front of them.

Kayden and Elijah were only a year apart at ten and eleven years old, but they could have been twins. They had the same white-blonde hair and blue eyes. Their faces were round and soft like their father's.

All the children stared at one another with curious expressions. Eddie's mouth fell open as he watched them. Frances soon lost interest and stepped to the side to see the shelves that filled the space under the stairs. They were filled with books.

"Do you have a dog?" Eddie blurted out.

"No," Kayden and Elijah said with laughs.

"Why don't you guys show Frances and Eddie around the house," Roger suggested. The boys nodded and waved at Frances and Eddie to follow. The four of them bounded up the long staircase. Harper realized she'd never even been up those stairs before.

When the kids were somewhere out of earshot, Roger asked, "Would you like some coffee?"

The three of them walked down the long hallway into the kitchen. The place looked like something out of a magazine or home renovation show. The marble countertops, the backsplash, and the cupboards were all white. The only contrast were the black accents, like the bar stools, the faucet, and appliances.

Roger went to the cupboard to retrieve three mugs. Even on his most casual days, he still dressed fancier than Harper ever dared to. To herself, and Levi and Olive, she called it Litigation Lawyer Chic. That day he wore a pair of pressed khaki pants with a light blue sweater.

He never seemed that old to Harper, even though he had almost a decade on her mother. From time to time the light would catch the grey hairs at his temple or the lines forming around the corner of his mouth.

Roger gave Harper a warm smile and asked, "How are you doing with everything? Hanging in there?"

Patricia looked like she might interrupt, so Harper started speaking quickly.

"I think Frances hates my guts, and I learned that five-year-old boys still need help wiping after they take a number two." She tried not to gag the way she had when Eddie called out to her for help the previous evening. Frances had been outside, getting some space from Harper, so she had no choice but to help. It never occurred to her when she agreed to help that it would involve bathroom issues. At least Frances sat in the bathroom while he bathed. It gave Harper a chance to work on some of her clients' designs.

Patricia cleared her throat, letting everyone know she had the floor before anyone else could speak, and asked, "What are you doing about child care? I'm sure your work wouldn't like it if you took too many days off."

Harper narrowed her eyes at her mother even though the statement shouldn't have come as a surprise. Patricia never took a day off work or night school. She never cut back her hours.

At least until she moved in with Roger. She went down to part time nursing. Despite what happened with Henry, Patricia thought she was safe for any future let down and disappointment. Harper couldn't believe her mother could be so easily fooled.

As if sensing the turn in the conversation, Roger cleared his throat and said, "It must be hard to juggle everything."

Despite it being only a handful of days, Harper had become so tired. She felt more exhausted in those three days since their arrival than she did after partying for four nights straight. Coming home after work to the kids in her space she couldn't have a beer or smoke some weed to relax. Instead, she spent the previous evening listening to Eddie talk about all the dogs he saw when they went on a walk and trying not to say something that would cause Frances to groan or roll her eyes. Harper had yet to learn how to avoid the reactions.

"We're good. Things are good. We're just taking it one day at a time."

"And, so what are you doing for child care?" Patricia asked, folding her arms across her chest.

Harper couldn't believe her mother was pushing so hard, like she wanted to hear that Harper struggled and failed. Would it make Patricia feel better to know that Harper was incapable, that she couldn't do it on her own without a man's money? It always seemed like Patricia was waiting for her to make mistakes so she could throw them back in her face.

"Olive is watching the kids while I'm working, but I'm cutting back how many clients I take on until the kids are in school in the fall," Harper told them.

Roger nodded. "It sounds like a good plan."

"Yeah. Once the kids have a permanent placement, I'll have to put in overtime until I build back the savings account though," Harper told them.

"You mean once they're here with us," Patricia corrected Harper.

"Sure. Whatever." Harper thought about bringing up how weird it was that Patricia was fighting to foster Henry Wilde's children, but she didn't have the energy for an argument. She would have to save the interrogation of her mother's intentions for another day.

"What about Olive's own siblings? Who is watching them if Olive is going out of her way to watch Frances and Edward?" Patricia went on.

As he filled all three mugs with coffee from the already brewed pot, Roger cleared his throat in an attempt to get Patricia's attention. Patricia glanced in his direction, but she didn't back down.

Harper held on to the kitchen island counter to keep balance, more emotionally than physically. With the kids upstairs, she didn't want to start yelling. "Bella and Bryson are staying with their aunt. Their mother is on another bender," Harper explained. "Just so you know, I am paying her for her time. I'm not taking advantage of her, if that's what you're thinking."

"Of course you're paying her. That girl is trying to put herself through university." Patricia shook her head like Harper had said something absurd.

Roger returned from the fridge with a bottle of milk and set it on the counter. He touched Patricia's arm before he said, "It sounds like you have things figured out."

"There's just one thing I wanted to run past you both," Harper told them. Bile rose in her throat while she waited for them to speak.

It had taken several pep talks with Maz and Olive to rationalize what she was going to ask. Maz told her that her mother was the reason she was in that predicament in the first place, so she should help watch the kids. Olive said that her mother kept bugging her about when she could see Frances and Eddie, so Harper was really doing Patricia a favour, and not the other way around.

It still made her feel itchy all over and made her t-shirt feel tight around the collar.

"Sure," Roger said between sips of his coffee. "Anything."

Harper wanted to run. "Saturday afternoons are my most profitable day at the shop. I'm booked solid for the next eight weeks."

Patricia folded her arms and arched her thin eyebrows as she waited. She already knew what was coming, but she planned on making Harper say it out loud.

Harper placed both hands on the cool marble countertop. "I wanted to know if you would mind watching the kids on Saturdays. It would be overnight, but twenty-four hours, tops. I'd drop them off at noon on Saturday and pick them up as soon as I wake up on Sunday."

Patricia stared at her.

Instant regret hit Harper.

"Of course," Roger said. "It will be good for them to start the transition to staying here once we're approved. Let them get to know us and get comfortable with us."

Harper gave a slow nod.

Patricia shifted her weight from one foot to the other and said, "You can always come after work and stay the night."

Harper opened her mouth and closed it again, unsure of how to respond. It felt like a trap.

Roger busied himself by grabbing a sponge from their sink and wiping the tiny droplet of coffee that had landed on the marble counter.

Before Harper found the words, the sound of four sets of feet came down the stairs, loud and fast. Elijah ran into the kitchen first and said, "We're going to swim."

"You can get changed in the pool house, but don't go near the pool until one of us is out there," Roger called after them.

Still stunned by her mother's offer, Harper took a second to realize what they had said. "They don't have suits."

Patricia smirked, like the awkward moment between them hadn't happened. "I'm prepared. I picked up a few sizes for them. They're already in the pool house."

Harper wished she had any other option than leaving the kids with them on Saturdays. The idea of having to see her mother every Saturday and Sunday seemed too much. It had been years since they had crossed paths that often, not since her mother moved out of Green Bridge.

"But back to the subject of child care, yes, we would love to take the children on Saturdays," Patricia said. She inched around the side of the kitchen island. "Would you like me to talk to them about it? Let them know the good news?"

Harper had lost the upper hand when it came to that

interaction. Not only did asking for help make her skin feel too tight, but her mother had thrown everything off by asking her to stay over on the weekend. She needed to get back on steadier footing.

"No, I'll head out there and talk to them," Harper said, abandoning the stool and the untouched coffee. She went to the huge windows that overlooked the sprawling backyard. Trees and well-placed shrubbery created natural barriers between the neighbours, giving almost total privacy. The pool shimmered in the afternoon sun.

Harper noticed Frances didn't go into the pool house with the boys. She sat cross-legged on a lounge chair in the sun, but hunched forward like she didn't have the energy to sit upright.

The three boys came running out of the pool house in matching swim trunks. All of them ran toward the water. Harper was about to knock on the glass, tell them to wait until she got down there, but they all stopped. Little Eddie missed running into Kayden by less than an inch.

By the hand gesturing and scowl on Frances' face, Harper knew she had told them to stop, to do what they were told. Roger's boys glared back at her, annoyed that she had ruined their fun, but they listened anyway.

Harper had worried how she would manage to take care of both of the children. Watching as Frances wagged her finger and then pointed at the house, some of the tension released in her muscles. Frances could take care of herself and that realization made the next couple months feel a little less bleak.

Harper strolled out to the pool and rolled up the sleeves of her t-shirt. She knew she should go back inside and get sunscreen for her shoulders, to protect all the artwork she collected on her body over the years, but the kids were waiting for her.

The moment Kayden laid eyes on her, they climbed into

the shallow end of the pool. Frances told Eddie to stay on the shallow side and reminded him that he had no idea how to even float.

"You're not going to swim?" Harper asked as she sat on one of the other loungers.

Frances picked at the cuff of her light wash jeans. "No."

"Do you want me to see if Patricia has a t-shirt for you to wear? It's pretty hot." Harper reached out to give the fabric of the long-sleeve shirt a tug, but Frances pulled away. She tucked her arms into her chest and turned her entire body.

It was hard to ignore that cue.

"Sorry," Harper said. "I just thought you'd want to have some fun."

"My dad died a week ago. Fun isn't really on the agenda," Frances said.

Harper bit the inside of her cheek. "Yeah, that can't be easy. Especially when you've been jostled from place to place and had to deal with so many strangers."

"Like you." Frances turned to look at her and asked, "But I guess this is where they're going to ship us off next? That's the whole plan?"

Harper glanced at the kids splashing in the pool. Kayden and Elijah were tossing toys for Eddie to duck into the water to grab. Each time he came up he sputtered and laughed. If Harper had been brought to that house as a kid, she wondered how different her life would have been. Maybe she would have gotten into a fancy art school and been able to focus on her sketches and painting instead of tattooing. As much as she loved her job, she wished she could create whatever she wanted, whenever she wanted.

Frances and Eddie had a chance at that life, before they were as jaded as she'd become. She glanced at the disapproving look on Frances' face and thought, 'At least Eddie anyway'.

"Would it be so bad?" Harper asked.

"You don't want to live here, so why should we want to?"

Harper raised her eyebrows at her. "You don't want to live here?"

"I don't know, but it doesn't matter, does it? I don't get a say in any of it," Frances shot back. "Just like I didn't get a say when they pulled me out of the last foster home to stick me with you."

Harper was offended. "They did tell you that was a temporary placement, right? I mean, the last place you were at."

"They all are," Frances said. "I'm not stupid. At least Eddie will get adopted. He will probably go to some family and I'll end up being moved around until I age out. That's what happens to teenagers."

Harper didn't know if being honest was the right thing to do, but if she were in Frances' place, she would have wanted the truth.

"They don't want to separate you. They hunted me down because they wanted you to stay together. That's the whole point of this. You were going to get placed in a group home and Eddie was going to stay with a family." Halfway through the statement, Harper realized she should have stopped talking. If the social worker didn't tell the kids, then she shouldn't have. It wouldn't do any good to break that news, but she didn't stop and the words were out there, hanging between them like the humidity.

Frances hung her head. "So, we just stay with you until they're ready to take us and then what? I assume your mother has no plans to adopt us?" Her volume was level, but her words were sharp.

"I don't know." Harper had no idea what Patricia intended. Those were details Patricia left out, like so much else. "Do you want to be adopted?"

Frances gave a sarcastic snort laugh. "No, but I'm also not

stupid. Did you know that like fifty percent of homeless people right now have been in foster care?"

"Shit, is that true?" Harper asked.

Frances was not done. She glared at Harper and said, "Basically all the kids that age out of the system, they have mental health issues."

"All?"

"Like seventy percent."

Harper's stomach became uneasy. "You're just a walking Google search, huh?"

Frances rolled her eyes. "Just so you know, if Eddie doesn't get adopted, it's because you ruined his chances. That family might have wanted him and instead he got stuck with someone who couldn't care less." She stood up and in a perfect, movie-esque storm off, she went back into the house, making sure to slam the door behind her.

Eddie called out to Harper to watch him before he crouched under the water's surface to grab a pink weighted tube. He popped up waving it around and yelling, "Did you see?"

"Yeah," Harper shouted back. "Good job, dude."

Harper couldn't believe it never crossed her mind to ask Patricia about her intentions for the long term. For all she knew, Frances could be right. The kids could have been better off staying in the system so they could find a permanent place to land.

"Watch me, Harper!" Eddie called out again.

Harper watched as he bounced in and out of the water, hoping she didn't step up only to ruin their lives.

CHAPTER SEVEN

Saturday nights at the Onyx had become a staple. Each Saturday night, after closing up Silver Sparrow, Harper showered, made herself cute, and headed out to drink and dance. The music wasn't her thing, not enough punk influence for her liking, but she loved being in the middle of the dance floor with a drink in her hand. Nothing could beat swaying and shaking it with her friends, with Levi. She felt loved when her friends would scream songs along with her or hug her or tell her they were having the best time. For a while, she could pretend life was always that simple.

She'd never been to the Onyx while single, though. The dance floor felt different when she knew she couldn't summon Levi to press his body against hers and sway to the music. She excused herself from the guy she'd been dancing with and headed to the bar.

The friends she'd come with, Ella and Faith, were flirting with a couple of men who were visiting from Ghana. At first, Harper stuck around and joined in on the conversation, but it didn't take long to realize they asked her questions only to be polite. It didn't bother her to be alone, so she gave them space.

While standing in line, waiting for yet another double whiskey soda, a man slid up next to her. He touched her arm to get her attention, and asked, "Are you drinking alone?"

The man at the bar was dressed in a full suit and tie, unlike the rest of the clientele, who were more casual. His undone top buttons showed off dark chest hair against his fair skin. His grin was wide and lopsided. He looked to be in his mid-thirties and very intoxicated.

Harper covered her drink with her hand as she picked it up, letting the straw poke out between two of her fingers. She took a long sip of it and stared at him, saying nothing, but waiting for the inevitable.

She knew men like that. Straight-laced men would come to the club and see her with her tattoos and her piercings. They made up ideas about her at first glance. Some of the men were smooth about it. They would chat and flirt and wait until she was drunk enough to ask her if she'd ever been with more than one man at a time or if she'd ever had sex in public. Other men didn't even buy her a drink before they asked her if she was 'a freak in bed'. One time, a guy came up to her and offered her three hundred dollars for a shirtless picture. Maz took a picture of herself on Harper's phone, sent it to the guy, and they spent the night drinking on his dime.

"You wanna take this party somewhere else?" the man in the suit shouted over the music.

"No," Harper said, glancing back at her friends. They would leave with the guys they met. If she left that night, she decided, it would be on her own.

"I have cocaine," he told her, his eyebrows bobbing as he said it; His cheesy grin only getting bigger.

He had no tact. She couldn't tell if he was behaving like a cop, or like someone who didn't worry about the consequences life might toss his way.

Harper tried to imagine how she would handle a post-cocaine tailspin with two children in the house. She'd never be able to drag herself from Green Bridge to White Oaks after that.

"My hotel is right across the street."

That made up her mind. But before she could say no, he leaned in and whispered, "I'm not normally into girls with so many tattoos."

Harper stepped back and shook her head. "I'm good. You have a good night, alright?"

The goofy smile disappeared. His eyes narrowed. "What do you mean you're good?"

"I mean, I'm just going to go back to my friends," Harper told him. She went to step around him, but he grabbed her arm. His grip was so tight she could feel the way his fingers dragged her skin as she tried to get away.

"Let me go," she warned him.

He laughed, amused, but his grip stayed firm.

Harper tipped out her drink, letting it spill down the front of the man's pants. He dropped her arm and she jumped out of his way in case he tried to reach for her again.

"You stupid bitch," he shouted at her, trying to remove as much of the drink as possible by brushing it away. Someone else stepped in, putting themselves between Harper and the man as if to shield her. She wanted to push them away, to finish what she started.

Then she realized who the broad back belonged to.

Those first seconds, before he turned, were a battle in Harper's mind. She wanted to kiss him, jump on him, wrap her legs around his waist, and beg him to never leave her again. She also wanted to tell him he was an asshole for not texting her back.

"What the hell are you doing here?" Harper shouted at Levi.

The man in the suit opened his mouth, ready to continue

the conversation, but Levi spread his hand wide and palmed the guy's face. A few women dancing nearby saw the whole thing and giggled. Another man in a suit, slightly older and less sweaty looking, grabbed him the way he grabbed Harper. The second man pulled him away, saving him from what could have been a fight. Levi never started a fight, but he never backed down either.

He turned to face her, his arms tense and flexed. His chest was puffed up, still ready for a confrontation. Harper ignored all of that.

Seeing him there, it caused her chest to tighten. She knew that he'd been with his parents to get away from her, but he must have known she would be at the Onyx. If he decided he wanted nothing to do with her, he wouldn't be there.

She worried about what Levi's mother said about her in their week together. She'd never been a big fan of her or their relationship. On multiple occasions, she warned them both that they were going to get hurt. She may have said they were both going to get hurt, but she narrowed her eyes at Harper each time. Harper had been deemed the villain in Levi's story.

Turned out his mother had been right.

"What are you doing here?" Harper shouted at him since he hadn't answered her the first time.

He tipped his chin to the edge of the dance floor, where one of his cousins and a few of his friends were kind of dancing, but mostly chatting. He touched her. His calloused fingers were rough against the soft skin of her inner wrist. Harper yanked her arm away, but not before relishing in his touch for the count of five.

"You knew I'd be here."

"Of course."

"You didn't think to call me first, give me a heads up. You could at least have answered one of my text messages,"

Harper kept going. She wanted to stop, but she was so angry at him and he needed to know how much.

"You were already here when we decided to come. I planned to stay out of your way," he told her.

Harper didn't know what to say to that. She hated how awkward she felt around him. Things between her and Levi had never been uncomfortable before. Not when they first met, not the first date, and not the first time they had sex. They always had a kind of ease she never thought possible with another person.

At first, she doubted they could ever love each other since there seemed to be no fire burning between them. It had been Levi who made her realize that she didn't have to be hurt or jealous or scared in a relationship. The fact that they didn't yell at each other and throw things when they disagreed, or assumed that every time they were in different places that something bad was happening, was new to her. It took some adjusting to what a non-toxic relationship meant. Levi had given her space and time to realize it.

At least he'd thought had.

"Sorry I didn't text you back."

Harper raised her eyebrows to let him know he should have. "It was the least you could have done after ruining my birthday."

Levi pressed his lips together and looked away. "I regret it."

A seed of hope took root in Harper's chest. She took a deep breath while trying to find the right words to say, the ones that would offer some sort of compromise. Like, once Frances and Eddie were with her mom, Levi could start spending more nights at her place. Maybe then she would be able to work up to having him move into her apartment. Moving somewhere else, it was too big of a leap, but if he could start off smaller…

Levi let out a sigh, his chest relaxing. "I mean, I regret how it happened and when, but I keep reminding myself it's for the best."

The little seed of hope shrivelled up. Her whole body felt like it began withering into itself. She wrapped her arms tighter around her body and said, "For the best?"

"We're in different places in life," Levi told her. He smiled, but there was nothing happy about its presentation. "I don't want to push you to move at my pace. I guess you're still figuring out what you want and that's good, it's healthy."

The thing that Harper loved most about Levi was his sensitive nature. Unlike all her past boyfriends, he expressed things that he liked and loved. He talked about the things that pained him and the way he felt when he dealt with loss. She envied him for that.

At that moment, she also hated it. If he had been like every other guy she'd dated, she could have offered to blow off their friends and have sex in the back of his truck and everything would have been fine.

A couple, grinding their bodies together to the music, bumped into them. Harper was knocked into Levi. She put her hands on his chest. He hadn't felt the hit the way she had. He's always been sturdier than she was.

"I'm sorry everything happened the way it did," Levi whispered to her. "I never meant to hurt you."

She let out a long sigh and said, "I don't want to talk about this anymore. I think I'm gonna go."

"You want a ride home?"

"I'll find my own way."

Levi rolled his eyes and pulled the keys from his pocket.

WITH A BROWN BAG OF FAST FOOD IN HAND, HARPER STROLLED over to the truck where Levi sat on the tailgate at the back of the parking lot. She laid out napkins on the truck's bed before setting down Levi's onion rings and burger.

"No mustard, extra onions, and I had them toast the bun a second time since I know you don't like how soft theirs is," Harper told Levi as she hoisted herself up to sit down next to him, the food between them.

"You didn't need to do that."

Harper shrugged. She had no idea what to say. The drive had been horrible. Levi didn't say anything, giving her space to talk, but she wouldn't take it, desperate for him to say something.

As much as she wanted to turn down the ride, take a cab or a ride share, she knew they needed to get the awkwardness out of the way. It had to be better than the first time they talked or spent time around each other being at Silver Sparrow without being able to hash things out.

"Are you dating anyone?" Harper asked him between bites of her fry.

Levi almost choked on his burger. He finished swallowing and said, "In the week that I've been visiting my family? No. I'm not dating anyone."

"I wouldn't be mad if you did," Harper told him, though even the thought of it made her chest burn.

He smirked and said, "That's such a lie. You've never been able to hide your true emotions when you're drunk."

Harper shook her head. "I'm not even that drunk."

"Tell your face that." He turned away and stared across the half-empty parking lot. A few cars came and went after grabbing food. When they first arrived there had been a group of teenagers hanging around with music blasting from their cars, but they wrapped up the night before Harper went inside to order.

They'd never parked in some parking lot and relaxed on his tailgate after a night out. When they did stop to pick up food, they always rushed back to one of their apartments instead.

It was a reminder of how things had changed. They were being friendly, but not too friendly.

"How are you coping with your dad's death?" Levi asked her. "I can imagine it's a lot to process."

Harper shrugged. "Not for me. Probably for the kids, but I've been told I'm not allowed to talk about it."

"Who told you that?" Levi asked.

"Frances. The oldest one. She basically said my dad abandoned me for a reason, so I don't get to speak about him with her." Harper set down her fries and picked up the burger. She unwrapped it, took a bite, and said, "So, that's about how fun things have been this week."

"I really doubt she meant that."

Harper let out a non-humorous laugh. "Frances seems pretty serious about it. She has no plans to get to know me while she's staying here. The minute I get back from work, she goes into her room and the little one follows me around until Frances puts him to bed."

Levi fiddled with the straw of his drink.

"I know what you're thinking," Harper told him. "I'm cold and shut off and it's my fault she doesn't want to talk to me. Stop judging me."

"I'm not judging you. That's not what I'm thinking at all. I'm thinking about how it must be tough to parent when no one parented you."

Harper sighed. "I guess pity is better than loathing. Marginally."

He chuckled. "I'd prefer to call it empathy."

Harper met his eyes. It had become a natural reaction to reach out and touch him, to kiss him, to expect to be held by him. She wondered how long it would take until that feeling went away. She worried it might never and she would have to live with the knowledge she brought it all on herself.

Levi turned away first. "How are you managing work and the house and the kids?"

"Olive is there when I'm working and if I buy groceries she cooks dinner, so that's helping. The kids are pretty self-sufficient though," Harper explained. "Frances gets them ready every day and does their laundry. So, it's not bad."

Levi's eyes shifted from side to side, like he had no clue where to look.

"Now you're judging me," Harper said, her tone harsh.

Levi shrugged. "A little."

"Why?"

Levi hooked his head.

"Come on. Spit it out."

He took a long time to exhale. He even took a sip of his drink before he answered. Harper wanted to shake it out of him.

"It's like something your mom has said about you," Levi told her.

Harper stared at him.

"You've even complained about how she bragged about you being an old soul and how sometimes she forgot she had a kid because you took care of stuff," Levi told her.

"Yeah, but at least I don't forget that they're there," Harper snapped at him, dropping the last half of her burger into the empty fast food bag, annoyed.

"Harper," Levi said.

He reached out to touch her and, as much as she wanted him to, she inched away. If his skin touched hers, she'd forgive him in an instant.

He of all people should know how much an accusation like that would hurt her. He was supposed to be the emotional one of the two of them, the empathetic one, the understanding one. Did he not think how much something like that would cut her to her core?

"I'm gonna get home on my own," Harper told him,

hopping off the tailgate. She pulled the phone from her bag and opened the app to order a ride.

"Don't be ridiculous," he told her. "We're going in the same direction."

Just to prove him wrong, she typed her mother's address into the 'To' field of the app, and said, "Nope. We're really not."

CHAPTER EIGHT

It only took fifteen minutes to get from the burger place to Patricia and Roger's house. It didn't give Harper enough time to calm down before arriving. She sat in the back of the car bouncing her leg while the driver watched her on and off in the rearview mirror. She wanted to snap at him, but Harper knew better than to pick a fight with a man while alone in his car.

"Who are you meeting?" the driver asked as he stopped in front of Roger's gate.

"No one," Harper lied. "I live here."

He did a double take, trying to make sense of her whole vibe living in a community like that. Harper glared at him and shut the car door harder than she needed to. She stomped her way up to the gate's keypad to let herself in.

When Patricia and Roger finally got engaged, they gave Harper her own code for the house and gate. It would be her unique code, they explained to her. Patricia let her know that they could see when she came and went based on that code. It was the first time Harper had ever taken advantage of it.

The house was silent as she entered. Without turning any lights on, she slipped off her shoes and dropped her bag on top of them. The plan had been to sneak into the house and pass out on the overstuffed couches in the family room. But she was too angry to sleep at that moment.

When she reached the bottom of the stairs, her feet carried her up them.

Harper hated that Levi could be right. In so many other ways, she'd worked hard not to turn into her mother. She got herself on birth control as soon as her first boyfriend suggested they have sex. She made sure that she created a sense of stability for herself that didn't involve men taking care of her. If she wanted to have kids, which was not in her plan for the future, she would make sure her life was stable so she could focus on them, care for them, raise them so that they didn't feel alone in the world.

Those kids weren't hers. She didn't owe them her life.

But, she realized as she reached the second floor, she had agreed to take on their care. If she had made that promise, she needed to follow through.

The short hallway to the right of the stairs was dark, meaning Roger and Patricia were sleeping. A soft glow of light came from one of the bedrooms at the end of the hallway to the left. Harper inched along the hardwood floors, hoping not to wake anyone else. Two of the bedroom doors to the left were open, light coming from the first. She reached it to find Frances and Eddie standing on the blue rug in the middle of a pretty large, almost entirely white room. Even the bed and dresser were white. Only the bedding and blinds had colour, navy blue like the carpet.

Eddie struggled to pull a pyjama shirt over his head while Frances balled up sheets and another pair of Eddie's pyjamas.

"Hey," Harper whispered, startling both Eddie and Frances.

Frances dropped the sheets she held and put a hand to her chest.

Eddie's face contorted like he might scream, but only for a

second. At the sight of her, he ran over and slammed his body against her. "You're here."

"I am. What's going on?" Harper asked, glancing at the stripped bed and the towel on the mattress.

Frances glared at her. "Are you drunk?"

Harper didn't expect to be called out. Not by the kids, anyway. She expected her mother to be the one to do that. "I had a few drinks."

"A *few* too many."

Harper ignored her. "What are you doing?"

Eddie started to cry. "I peed. I'm sorry."

Frances sighed and picked up the sheets again.

Harper patted his head, unsure of what else to do, and said, "Hey, it's okay. It happens."

"Frances said you'd get mad, so we couldn't tell."

Harper could feel her composure falling apart. She looked at Frances and asked, no longer keeping her voice down, "Is that true? Did you tell him that?"

Frances didn't say anything and didn't make eye contact. That alone spoke volumes.

"Our last foster lady got angry and made me sleep on a garbage bag. No blanket," Eddie told Harper.

Harper cursed under her breath, and Eddie said nothing. She realized he might be worried about why she was swearing, if it might be directed at him. Crouching down in front of him, Harper said, "I'm not mad at you. I'm mad at that lady for doing that."

"You don't have to deal with this," Frances told Harper. "Go sleep it off. I got this."

The offer was tempting. She really could walk downstairs and pass out on the couch without having to worry. Frances didn't seem new to the situation.

But then Harper would be acting like her mom, the way Levi accused her of behaving. She hated that he'd been right all along. The whole time she kept thinking she needed to stay out of their way and get through the four to six months.

It would never be that simple. Harper wasn't a way station on the trip to the next phase of their lives. They were linked to her, regardless of where they went next. Harper wouldn't be able to ignore the fact that she had blood relatives out in the world. Especially if they ended up living with her mother.

"Does this happen often?" Harper asked.

"Every couple nights," Frances admitted.

"Was this happening at my place too?"

Frances shrugged, which meant yes. She had been taking on all those tasks on her own without asking for help. The fact that Harper didn't realize there were dirty sheets piling up or that Frances had been doing laundry behind her back was alarming.

Her breathing quickened at the thought of Frances and Eddie taking care of themselves. She had been that girl, doing her own laundry, making her own meals, making sure not to disturb the adults. The adults in her life expected it from Harper and she hadn't wanted to let them down.

Harper had to be present and focused and be the person her mother could never be for her.

The anger and frustration she experienced over what Levi said had been a defence mechanism, she realized.

Eddie's chin quivered. She didn't want him to cry. She didn't know how to deal with tears, so she reached out and pulled him into her. He smelled like baby powder-scented shampoo and minty toothpaste. She squeezed him and whispered that it wasn't a big deal, that he was okay.

When he no longer looked on the verge of a meltdown, Harper escorted Eddie to the bed and sat him down, then put her hand out to Frances. "Hand those to me."

Frances turned her entire body to keep the sheets away from her. "I said no. I can handle it."

"I didn't say you couldn't, but let me wash them. You two can go back to bed," Harper told her.

Frances' whole body tensed as Harper took a step forward. Her mouth opened and closed like she planned to object, but couldn't find the words. Her slight bend in the knees made it appear she was ready to run away from Harper at a moment's notice.

"Frances," Harper said, "I'm just going to take them and toss them in the wash. I'm already going downstairs to sleep on the couch."

Frances still didn't move, so Harper walked around her and took the bundle of bedding from her hand. It took a little force to slip it from her grasp. With the laundry in hand, Harper reached down and planted a kiss on the crown of Eddie's head.

"You guys get back to sleep. If you need me, I'll be in the family room," Harper told them as she took another glance around for leftover clothes to put in the load. She walked out of the room to the sound of Frances telling Eddie she would stay with him if he wanted.

Harper tried not to imagine how much effort Frances had been putting in behind her back. A few things clicked in her mind, like how she hadn't made either of them breakfast since they arrived. It had been Frances who got Eddie into the bath and brushed his teeth.

Harper walked into the laundry room at the back of the house on the main floor. As she dropped the bundle on the ground, to prepare the washing machine, she thought about how she would make it work, how she could keep her job and the money coming in while making kids a priority. Her mother made it seem impossible for a single woman to do both. It occurred to her, as she pulled open the washing machine door, that her mother deserved more empathy. Holding down a job, night school, and a kid while trying to find time to date. Her mother deserved a little respect for doing all those things.

Maybe Harper needed to put some of her anger toward her mother aside.

From the grey cabinet, she snatched up a few laundry pods from the glass jar and tossed them into the machine. She reached down to grab the bedding and noticed that it wasn't only Eddie's clothes in the pile of sheets. A few of Frances' things had made it into the pile as well. A pair of jeans and a sweater with a tank top still stuck inside. When Harper pulled the tank top out, she noticed the streaks of red on the white fabric. Blood. It didn't look like anything else.

All of the streaks of blood were on one side of the tank top. They were too straight, too symmetrical to be from a fall or from wiping blood from somewhere else. She had seen blood patterns like that before. Men and women also walked into Silver Sparrow every day hoping to find someone to cover the scars that once made crimson stains on clothes just like that.

Trying to drunkenly rationalize it, Harper realized it could be something else. Her assumption came from her bias, from knowing people who had done such things to their own body.

"She's not cutting herself," Harper said out loud, hoping to believe it.

She couldn't come straight out and ask Frances. It had been a few years since she was a teenager, but she knew what the reaction would be. Deny, deny, deny. That would be followed by an attempt to hide the situation better than before. More secrets wouldn't help the situation.

If Harper wanted to discuss it, if she wanted to do something about it, she needed proof.

Unable to look at it any longer, she shoved everything into the washing machine and turned it on. Resting her back against it, Harper let out a long sigh.

CHAPTER NINE

While Patricia berated her, Harper stared across the kitchen island at Frances, who was helping all three of the boys pick a show to watch on the massive television in the family room. Being a moody teenager didn't mean she was hurting herself. Harper wondered if those blood patterns could be from anything else.

"It's just absolutely unacceptable behaviour to show up here drunk," Patricia scolded as they dished up breakfast for all four of the children. "In Roger's house."

Her mother was right. If Harper had been sober, it never would have occurred to her to go to Roger and Patricia's house. She'd never felt welcome enough to show up unannounced. She'd been so angry at Levi that she hadn't thought it through.

Despite the pounding at the base of her neck and the unease in her stomach from the alcohol, Harper decided she would take over breakfast that morning. She feared the kids would ask for eggs, something her nausea wouldn't be able to handle, so she made chocolate chip pancakes, using a mix from the cupboard, and a pack of peameal bacon she found in the fridge. When Frances came into the kitchen to fix something for herself and Eddie, Harper shooed her out.

If the kids were going to live with Patricia long term, Harper wanted to set them up with the expectation that children were supposed to be cared for by the adults in their lives. They didn't have to fend for themselves and make all the hard decisions. Even though it seemed like Frances had already been carrying that burden for a while.

"Can you cut this shit out? I said I'm sorry," Harper said as she turned to flip another set of pancakes. She had other things on her mind, more important things that her mother's concerns about her drinking. "You offered to take the kids for the night and I needed to blow off some steam, so I had a few drinks."

"But then you came home intoxicated," Patricia said in a loud whisper. "It's a good thing that our foster application has already started. The sooner we have custody, the better."

Patricia had woken Harper at five-thirty in the morning and yelled at her for smelling like a brewery, and for sneaking into the house unannounced. Not only did her mother wake her for no reason, but she scolded her? After all these years, when Harper no longer needed a parent, Patricia decided to take on a motherly role? It came a little too late and felt like a slap in the face.

Harper bit the inside of her cheek. If she fought back, if she argued with her mother, it would turn into a whole thing. The kids were in the family room that sat off the kitchen. If it escalated, they would be able to hear. No matter how much she wanted to tell her mom off, it was only the first day of her new mission to put them first. She couldn't back down from it already.

"I'm asking you nicely to leave it alone," Harper told her mother in an actual hushed voice. "I'm trying really hard not to pack up my stuff and walk out of here for the kids' sake, alright? Just drop it."

Patricia slammed down the tiny knife she was using to cut strawberries. The kids went silent in the other room.

Harper turned around, spatula in hand, and said, "I shouldn't have come here after drinking. I get that. But if you're going to keep going on about this while the kids are around, I won't be bringing them back here."

Patricia raised her eyebrows. "You won't be bringing them back here? Who do you think is going to take care of them? Remember, I'm the one that stepped up to take care of them. You're just filling in for me."

Harper's head snapped in the direction of the children. The boys were chatting about Spiderman while pointing at the television. Frances seemed to be involved in her new phone. None of them showed any signs of hearing what Patricia said.

There were so many things Harper wanted to shout back to her mother in that moment. Any empathy she'd drunkenly developed the night before was gone. Those feelings were replaced with all the years of anger and frustration, the aching feeling that she had been abandoned by yet another parent.

Yet that parent wanted to take on someone else's kids.

Harper placed a hand on her stomach and reminded herself to breathe. After swallowing down all the resentment, she focused on the situation and nothing else when she said, "Stop. If you want to be angry at me, be angry at me, but don't do it while they're in the room. They have been through enough."

Patricia closed her eyes and shook her head before saying, "You think you know so much about children and parenting. You have no clue how hard it is."

If they hadn't had an audience of minors, Harper would have gone off. Instead of shouting at Patricia out loud, Harper ran through all the things she wanted to say. All the empathy Harper had for her mother the night before had become close to impossible to muster up in that moment. She bit her lip so as not to ask why she swooped in to rescue Frances and Eddie when she had no time for her own daughter.

Harper turned back to the pan to flip the two chocolate chip pancakes, trying not to scream and storm out. One of them had to be the bigger person. Harper wished that role didn't fall to her to fill time and time again.

Patricia sucked in a breath, which Harper knew meant she hadn't finished getting everything off her chest. Putting the spatula down far too hard on the stovetop, causing a plastic cracking sound, Harper turned toward the living room.

"Breakfast is ready," she called out, even though she hadn't made enough food for herself.

The three boys came running into the kitchen and tossed themselves into the bench seat of the breakfast nook. They laughed with each other as they fought for the middle.

Even though the anger toward Patricia still ached in her chest, Harper thought about how nice it would be for Eddie to have Roger's boys around for him to grow up with. The kids hadn't said much about their lives with Henry, but she got the impression they were on their own a lot. Patricia and Roger could offer a full household.

The thought caused a burning in the pit of Harper's stomach.

Frances came into the kitchen with the sleeves of her sweater pulled over her hands. All Harper's self pity and anger dissipated in that moment as she stared at the way Frances tugged at her sleeves. There were signs that her theory was right.

Unaware, France looked at all the pancakes stacked on top of each other and asked, "You can cook?"

Patricia watched Harper, waiting for her reaction. The statement was one of the least offensive things Frances had said to her since her arrival. It almost made Harper laugh.

Instead, she shrugged. "You can be the judge of that. Can you take that plate over to the table?"

Frances nodded, grabbing the pancake-filled plate and the bowl of cut strawberries even though she hadn't been asked.

Harper went back to pouring batter into the frying pan and ignored the way her mother huffed as she went to the table to join the boys. When Harper turned around to prepare her own plate, she found Frances taking a seat at the kitchen island.

"You don't want to sit with Eddie?" Harper asked.

Frances shook her head, but said nothing.

Harper turned her attention back to the pancakes, watching the edges bubble before she flipped them over. When she served up two for herself, she turned off the stove and asked Frances, "Would you mind if I sat with you?"

"I don't care."

The two of them sat at the kitchen island, eating in silence while the boys talked about a video game. Kayden told Eddie that he needed to try it when he came over the next Saturday.

Harper wondered if it were that easy. She did one simple thing like tossing laundry into the machine and she was rewarded with less attitude? It seemed like a win.

"Sorry about last night," Harper said, keeping her voice low so Patricia wouldn't hear it. "I shouldn't have come back here after drinking. I gotta get used to this adult in charge shit. I mean, stuff."

"It's fine."

"It's not. I shouldn't have done it. Next time, if I'm going to go out and have some drinks, I'll make sure I arrange it so you guys don't have to be caught in the middle of it," Harper said, and she meant it. "You both have been through enough with your dad and I don't want to add to the list of things you have to process."

"I'm processing fine."

"Are you?" Harper asked, wondering if this was her lead

into the blood stains she found. If she had, it worked out way better than she'd been expecting.

Frances put down her fork and asked, "You're not going to drop this, are you?"

Harper sighed. She didn't want to push it too much too fast. "I'll drop it."

Frances picked up her fork and cut into her pancake. "Then I'll accept your apology."

Harper smiled as she stuffed a large piece of peameal bacon into her mouth. Even though Frances agreed only to shut her up, it didn't end in a storm off. If she made too big of a reaction, she might scare Frances off, and she had a feeling that her emotions were walking a pretty tight line already.

"Well, thanks. I appreciate that," Harper said after she swallowed.

By the way Frances shifted in her seat, Harper worried an uncomfortable silence might fall. To diffuse it, she asked, "Is there anything you guys need to do before the week starts? Any groceries we should buy or clothes that need to be washed?"

Would it show on her face that she found something on the clothes she washed the night before? A jolt of concern shot through Harper, causing her to sit up straighter. Had mentioning washing clothes been a bad idea?

"Do we have to go straight back to the apartment after this?" Frances asked.

"Is there something you wanna do?" Harper asked.

Frances gave a head shake that Harper assumed meant she had nothing in mind.

"There's a park that runs from here down to this diner I haven't tried before," Harper offered. "It's gonna be hot, but there's lots of trees for shade and it runs by a river."

The thought of walking through the hot, sunny park with her hangover made Harper want to say no, but she had no idea what else to do with them that wouldn't cost her a lot of money. The single park in Green Bridge was not an inviting place, even during the day.

"How about this? When we're ready to go, why don't we pack up and walk through the park, grabbing lunch on the other side, then we can catch the bus from the diner back home. How does that sound?" Harper asked.

"Yeah," Frances said, with her mouth full. "Let's do that."

Despite the bloody clothes, her mother's scolding, and the slight throbbing at the base of her skull, Harper sensed her goal to do more, be more present, was going to be a good thing.

Harper had been too lost in her own thoughts to notice Roger coming into the kitchen holding a vibrant pink bag. She couldn't ignore it when he placed it in front of her, some of the glitter from the words 'Happy Birthday' fell onto her plate.

"What's this?" Harper asked, confused. She looked at Patricia, who refused to meet her eye.

Roger smiled. "Your birthday gift. Your mother wanted to give it to you earlier, but with everything going on we thought it better to wait."

Harper turned to look at her mother again, looking for answers. She received nothing in return.

"Oh. Cool." Harper took a second to remember the right thing to say. "Um… Thank you. Both."

Harper knew better than to open it in front of everyone. The pink bag told her she might have to fake a smile, but the lack of sleep would make that impossible. At home, without an audience, she could at least take a moment to make her thank you text message convincing.

Patricia didn't acknowledge the present or the thanks. Harper couldn't figure out if she felt relieved or annoyed.

While searching for recommendations for pull-up diapers or some alternatives for Eddie, Harper glanced up at the pink bag on the coffee table. Frances had carried it from the bus after Harper got up, leaving it on the seat.

The bag dropped glitter all over the house. Harper told herself she would sweep up after the kids went to bed, but exhaustion had set in from working ten hours the day before, from drinking too much, from dealing with everything else that had happened in the previous twenty-four hours. The dishes had piled up in the sink. Her own clothes hadn't been washed and she would be dipping into her worn out, emergency underwear stash within a day or two.

The glitter would have to wait.

Harper set down her laptop and stared at the bag. It occurred to her a number of times that her mother hadn't bought the gift at all. Had Roger realized Patricia forgot her own daughter's birthday and run out to save the day? The pink bag didn't seem like something Roger would have chosen for her. It would be more like Patricia to get a pink bag even though Harper only liked pink on her nails and in her hair.

The present made her uncomfortable. They hadn't exchanged gifts in Harper's adult life. She couldn't remember the last time her mother had given her a gift. Some time before she turned eleven they stopped, but she couldn't pinpoint exactly when.

She had to open it. The longer she left it sitting on the table the longer she would think about it. She didn't want to think about it anymore.

Her phone vibrated. Olive.

> can i come back? mom's brought friends over and the kids are with my aunt.

> You don't have to ask.

Harper got up from the couch and headed out of the apartment into the foyer. She double checked for the baseball bat she and her neighbours kept by the door. When she confirmed it was within reach, she pushed open the front door and watched as Olive came speed walking down the sidewalk.

"You alright?" Harper asked when Olive made it up the stairs.

Her cheeks were flushed. She was still wearing her uniform from Kabir's Kitchen: a white button-up shirt with black pants and a black apron. As she came through the door, she took off the backpack weighing down her shoulders and said, "Fine. Angelica's just in a real state tonight."

Harper locked the door behind her and they walked into the apartment together. They grabbed a can of pop from the fridge before heading into Harper's room. She closed the door over and said, "You can sleep in here if you want. I'll take the couch."

They kept their voices low as they spoke.

"Nah, I'll take the couch. I'll make breakfast in the morning." Olive dug into her backpack and pulled out a change of clothes.

"I can make breakfast," Harper said. "You can sleep in."

"I won't sleep in, but you can make breakfast." Olive smiled at Harper before pulling off her shirt and slipping on a fresh one.

Harper grabbed the dirty one and said, "I can toss that in with my wash, whenever I get around to it."

"Would you like me to do laundry when you're at work on Tuesday?"

"No. I hired you to watch the kids, not be my maid," Harper told her, snatching Olive's work pants too.

"And yet, you could just ask me to do it as a favour."

"Nope."

Olive laughed and tossed herself onto the bed. "So stubborn."

Harper stuck out her tongue and said, "Your purple is so faded. I have the rest of the bottle under the sink. Do you want me to do your hair?"

Olive draped an arm over her face and eyes. "Nah. I can do it this week sometime."

Harper flopped back onto the bed too and said, "My mom bought me a birthday gift."

Olive sat up. "What?"

"Or at least Roger said she bought it. Maybe he did."

"What is it? Is it like 'for you', but really for the kids? One of those situations?" Olive asked, eyes wide. "Because she's acting really weird about suddenly wanting to be a parent."

"Right?" Harper said with a sigh. "But no clue what it is. I didn't open it. It's sitting on the table."

Olive wasted no time. She pushed herself off the bed and went to get it. She came back in and said, "Pink glitter? Does she know how much you hate glitter?"

Harper sat up on her elbows. "It's already on literally everything."

"Open it." Olive sat on the bed again, placing the bag between them. More glitter tumbled off it onto the navy blue duvet cover.

"I don't know if I'm in the mood."

"If you don't open it now, you're going to put it off so long that you tuck it away and never look at it again. Like that box of your dad's stuff you have hidden in the back of your closet."

Harper gave her an over-the-top glare.

Olive laughed. "Open it."

Harper sat up and pulled out the pink tissue paper. More glitter fluttered onto the comforter. Inside was a black box. It had a small gold clasp on the front. Harper winced at the thought of jewelry. As much as she admired dainty rings and bracelets, she never thought they would suit her, that they wouldn't fit with her vibe. Instead, she opted for a cheap, fake gold necklace with a charm of ocean waves, even though she'd never seen the ocean and the necklace sometimes made her neck green.

The box was too heavy for jewelry. Harper set it on the bed while Olive shifted the bag to the floor. Inside the box was a stone in the shape of a rose. It was pink and black and came with a matching bowl that acted like a stand. Harper set it in her palm and held it up in front of them.

"What the hell am I looking at?" Harper asked with a single eyebrow arched.

"Rhodonite, I think," Olive said. "In the shape of a rose."

Patricia bought her a stone flower. Why? Harper turned it around in her hand looking for some clue of why her mother thought of her when buying it. It occurred to her again that maybe her mother had not bought it at all. Maybe Roger, a man without daughters, thought a pink stone flower would be the perfect gift.

"My mom bought me a pink, stone rose." Harper had to say the words out loud, so they could both take in the strangeness of the gift.

"I would say it's a crystal," Olive told her with a quiet giggle. "But it's a weird move on your mom's part."

Harper leaned across her bed to the windowsill her bed was pressed against. She set the stone rose on the sill and stared at it for a second.

"Is your mom going through some sort of midlife crisis?" Olive asked, also staring at the stone rose.

Harper let out a sigh. "I have no idea what's going on. I just keep waiting for her to tell me that the kids are actually hers and I just don't remember her pregnant with them or something. I don't know what to make of any of this."

"It's cute though," Olive said, before she yawned.

"Yeah," Harper said, reaching out to touch the cool stone. "It's cute."

Staring at the flower, Harper realized how enmeshed her and Patricia's lives had become since the children arrived.

When Patricia first packed up her things and moved out of Green Bridge, Harper had to give up hope that her mom might realize that she had been a good daughter, that she wanted to have her around. All the effort she'd put in hadn't been enough to make Patricia see her. Harper made peace with Christmas dinners and the occasional, obligatory text messages on Easter and Thanksgiving.

She didn't know if she could get her hopes up again. Another round of heartbreak from her mother would be too much to come back from.

CHAPTER TEN

For the third night in a row, Harper didn't make it back to bed after getting Eddie up to use the bathroom or change him out of the pull-ups that she bought online. The couch had become her second bed. When Eddie woke up each morning, sometime around six-thirty, he climbed over Harper and curled up behind her legs to watch television. She tried to go back to sleep, but even in the morning, despite the air conditioner unit working overtime, the place was too warm for cuddling. That third morning, she dragged herself off the couch to make breakfast hours before she wanted to wake up.

Harper leaned against the counter as she cut fruit for Eddie's breakfast. She yawned so long and hard, her head rolling back with exhaustion, that she had to set the knife on the cutting board for safety. If she planned on making it all the way through her workday and the two back-to-back clients, she would need a nap.

"Harper," Eddie whined from the living room. "I can't turn on the TV."

With her eyes still shut from the yawn, Harper asked, "Why not?"

"I can't find the button thing," he said, his words getting

higher pitched and more drawn out. The longer he went without the remote, the moaning would only get more intense. She stepped away from the counter and shuffled around the couch. At three-thirty that morning, she'd shoved the remote between the couch cushions when she was too tired to move it.

She retrieved it from the couch and stood up to hand it to him, but Eddie sat on his knees in front of the coffee table. He had pulled out one of her blank sketchbooks and pencil crayons she hadn't used in years. In the centre of the page, he drew what clearly depicted a dog next to a house. The dog was half the size of the house, but it impressed Harper to see it had full facial features and the house had windows and doors. While she had no clue what drawing milestones were for kids at five, it seemed like impressive work.

"You like to draw?" Harper asked him. She did a poor job masking the surprise in her voice.

"I want to colour," Eddie told her with a sigh. "I don't have my book."

Harper felt a pang of sadness about that. The two of them had left so much behind. The first week had been such chaos trying to get into a rhythm and figure things out, there hadn't been time to think about all the stuff that they had to abandon against their will. It was everything.

Harper wiped her hands on her oversized Black Flag t-shirt and crouched down in front of the coffee table. "Well, I don't work Mondays, so next Monday why don't we go to the store and pick up some stuff for you to colour and draw. Some of your own stuff."

"Okay," he said, bouncing on his spot.

"Here," Harper said, reaching for the sketchbook. "I can make some stuff for you to colour in. What do you want to colour?"

She reached into the bin of pencils and markets until she found a thick sharpie marker.

"Farm animals," Eddie yelled, pumping a little fist in the air as he did.

"I guess if you're up I have to be up too," Frances groaned from the bedroom.

Harper and Eddie looked at each other and laughed.

While Frances dragged herself out of bed and into the bathroom, Harper drew a barn near the top of the page. She put slightly oversized hay bales next to it. She was drawing lines on the roof when Eddie pointed at it and said, "No, not like that." He ran a finger over the lines as if trying to erase them.

"You don't want me to add texture to the roof?" Harper asked.

Eddie wrinkled up his nose and shook his head. "Leave it."

Amused, Harper moved on to drawing a cow. She had to stop twice to think about what cows looked like and how she could work the image to have fewer lines to make it easier to colour.

"Add a dog," Eddie said, touching a blank spot on the page. "And a horse."

"What about sheep?" Harper asked him. Sheep she could draw without having to think about it too much, especially at that time in the morning.

"And sheep."

By the time Harper finished drawing a very simple picture of a farm, adding little swooshes to signify grass, Frances walked into the living room and threw herself down on the couch. She looked at the sketchbook and said, "Did you draw that?"

"Yup."

"Like right now?"

If Frances was impressed or not, Harper had no clue. Her face gave no indication either way.

"Do you guys want me to make some sort of egg bake, or I

don't know what it's called. Like a bunch of eggs in a baking dish with veggies and maybe bacon."

Frances closed her eyes. "I can make my own breakfast."

"Just tell me what you want. I'll make it."

Frances sat up sharply and said, "Why are you being so weird? Why are you doing all these things?"

Harper stood up. "Making breakfast?"

"And doing our laundry and not letting us do our dishes," Frances told her. Her face puckered up like she'd tasted something sour.

"You guys have been through a lot and–"

Frances cut her off. "Oh god, did your mom tell you to say that? Patricia is constantly pitying us and being annoying. I don't want your pity."

Harper didn't want to argue. She was too tired to argue. "Fine. Make your bed."

Frances blinked. "What?"

"Every morning, make your bed and put your laundry in the hamper. Oh, and if you see that a garbage can is full, take the bag outside and put it in the bin," Harper told her.

"Even at night?" Frances asked, eyebrows raised.

This didn't occur to Harper. She shook her head. "No, if it's full at night, tell me and I'll take it out. Does that seem fair?"

Frances didn't make eye contact, didn't show any signs of annoyance or frustration. "Fine. That's fine."

An agreement had been reached, but Harper knew she couldn't ignore the comment about Patricia feeling sorry for them.

"But, about the pity thing. I wasn't pitying you. Calling out that you guys have been through some shit is just a fact. You know, sometimes it's good to talk about things," Harper said to Frances, but she gave Eddie's shoulder a squeeze so he would know she also meant him.

"You swore," Eddie said without even glancing up from his colouring page.

Harper smiled, but Frances was focused. She tipped her head to one side and asked, "Do you talk about things?"

A lightning bolt of panic hit Harper in the chest. Should she talk about her suspicions of Frances' self harm? Should she talk about how their dad abandoned her so she doesn't want to talk about him either? Should she talk about how her mother always treated her like a roommate and not a daughter? None of those were things she could bring up with the kids. She needed to be the adult in the situation. They needed to be the ones doing the talking.

"Did your dad ever draw or colour with you?" Harper asked Eddie, hoping that bringing him up without talking about their loss would make it easier to open up. Frances shook her head to show she disapproved of the conversation.

Eddie looked up at Harper and said, "No."

"What did you and your dad do together?" Harper asked him. She knew he must have taken them along on photography walks, as he called them, the way he'd done with her.

Photography had been Henry Wilde's biggest passion. He tried so hard to get Harper interested and would drag her from spot to spot hoping she would see things in thirds like he taught her. He would explain the golden hour to her repeatedly, hoping it would stick. Even though she had no desire to become a photographer, he bought her a camera that they couldn't afford, something her mother shouted about for hours when she found out. Henry would tell Harper she needed to develop her eye, look for beauty in the mundane. When she looked at sketchbooks or pencils in stores, he would tell her not to waste her time on drawing when she could capture the real world. Harper remembered a morning, not long before he left for good, he found Harper drawing in her schoolbook. He watched her for almost a full minute before saying, "What a waste."

Had he done the same to them?

"Did your dad ever take you on what he called photography walks?"

Frances' eyes shot up. "No."

The response surprised Harper. If he hadn't taken her, was it the mention of him or the mention of photography that interested her? Without directly asking, she went on, hoping to find out the answer. "He loved taking pictures. Of everything."

"My dad didn't like photography," Frances said.

"He used to," Harper told her. She had to wonder if her lack of interest had been so frustrating for him that he didn't bother to share that interest with his children. Had she ruined that experience for them? Had Frances missed out because of her?

"Well, it doesn't matter now, does it?" Frances said, trying to shut down the conversation. She took the phone from the pocket of her pyjama pants and focused her attention on that.

Harper didn't want to drop it. A nugget of information had been revealed and she wanted to dig it out. "What do you like taking pictures of?"

"I never said I did."

"Are you sure? Because I could take you to some cool places on Monday, after we get some colouring books for your brother," Harper told her.

"No, you draw them," Eddie said, tapping the sketchbook with his pointer finger.

Harper laughed and said okay, but her attention stayed on Frances. "So, wanna go to some cool places to take pictures?"

"No."

"Are you sure?"

Frances got up off the couch. "I'm going to clean my room." She stormed off and slammed the doors behind her.

The slamming didn't affect Harper in the least. She told Eddie he was doing a good job and went back into the kitchen to finish breakfast. The memory of Henry Wilde dragging her all around the city while telling her to capture the life she lived, stuck with her as she fried up eggs and made toast.

She'd been so desperate as a kid to have her father's attention. Even when he got frustrated that she couldn't see the lighting the way he could, she still followed him from location to location. Despite being yelled at for distracting him, like the last time they went out, Harper still nodded each time he told her to get her things. He was going to teach her to be a real photographer, he would say.

Then he left. He'd been so disappointed in her failure that he hadn't bothered to pass down his photography knowledge to his other children, even the daughter who seemed to have an interest in it. It was yet another thing the kids had lost.

As she set a plate of food in front of Eddie, as she told him she would draw more pictures while he ate, she wondered where she put the camera her father had bought her.

"Did your dad ever colour with you?" Harper asked while they ate around the coffee table.

With a mouthful of eggs, Eddie said, "No."

Harper pushed her food around the plate. "What did you guys do together?"

Eddie shrugged. "Daddy slept in the day time and he worked at night."

"What did you guys do together?"

"Watched football."

"That sounds like fun," Harper said to him, hoping it sounded sincere. Eddie stopped eating and stared at his plate for a minute. Harper realized she'd pushed too hard. She'd asked too many questions. She thought she heard a sniffle coming from the kids' bedroom, but she couldn't be sure.

CHAPTER ELEVEN

Until the kids came to stay with her, Harper cared very little for how many hours she put in at Silver Sparrow. Some days she would be there for ten or even twelve hours. If she didn't have her own work to do, she printed stencils for the other artists or swept the floors or answered phones. She loved being there.

That day, she rushed to get her station broken down and cleaned up after her last client. She still had social media to post and a design to work on the following day, but Olive was dropping Frances and Eddie off before she had to go to work.

"Hey," Levi's voice came from behind her. They had been avoiding each other at work after what happened the previous Saturday. They would pass each other in the break room or when in the store room, but they found every reason to leave a space if they were the only two there. It was an unspoken agreement that they were not ready to talk it out.

It seemed Levi had changed his mind.

"Maz wants to know if you can take another client today?"

A 'yes' almost popped out of her mouth without thinking.

She had become accustomed to taking on every client that came up. Clients were money. Money was freedom, especially with all the expenses she'd been accumulating.

For a brief second, she wondered if Frances would be able to watch her brother for a couple hours while she took the client. It would mean money to keep them in clothes and a roof over their heads.

Then it hit her. That's how her mother justified canceling plans and being gone all the time.

Harper shook her head. "Plans with the kids. I can't."

Levi gave her an approving smile before he leaned back, hollering to Maz that she'd have to schedule for another day. Harper went back to wiping things down, assuming Levi would leave, but he didn't.

Before she could ask what he wanted, Noah glided his wheelchair next to Levi and said, "I think someone forgot the rule that there's no kids in the goddamn shop."

Harper laughed, but ignored his annoyance. With the disinfecting wipe in her hand, she pointed at the stack of papers on the table and asked, "Could you take those sheets and crayons out to Eddie? I'll need another ten to fifteen minutes and I don't want them to bug you guys."

Levi reached for them, but stopped before handing them to Noah. He asked, "Did you make these?"

Harper didn't want to answer. She'd made them while on her break between clients, hiding out in her station, avoiding the awkward run-ins with Levi. To avoid eye contact, she went back to wiping down the tattoo chair.

"Look at this one," Levi said to Noah, passing the pages to him. "It's the shop. And this one is you."

Harper had run out of barn animals and dogs to draw. She created a cartoon version of the Silver Sparrow building in a traditional tattoo style. It inspired her to draw a few other places from the neighbourhood in the same way, like the rusted-out car that sat on an empty lot between two houses, as well as the house where Harper had her apartment.

"You got the PDFs? Can I print them out for my kids?" Noah asked.

Harper was taken aback by his expression. The raised eyebrows, the serious face; Noah was impressed. They weren't intricate or unique. He could have done something similar himself, if not better, and when she told him that, he shook his head.

Levi didn't look at her, but kept flipping through the pages.

"They're on my tablet," Harper said, nodding to the tablet charging right next to Levi. "Print them whenever you want."

"Nice." He swatted at Levi to give him the pages. He put them on his lap with the mega size box of crayons and wheeled his way to the front of the shop.

Levi didn't leave the doorway. He put his hands into the pockets of his jeans before taking them out again and folding his arms across his chest. Harper had to go back to cleaning because she sensed what would come next. Levi was working up to confronting her. Twice in a couple weeks. As much as she didn't want to have a 'talk' while they were at work, she had to commend him for dealing with things head-on.

"So," he said, after giving enough time for Noah to put some distance between them. "Should we talk about what happened?"

"Nah," Harper said. She focused on wiping the bend in the chair harder than she needed to. "We're good."

"I doubt that," Levi said. "You were always the one that pushed me to confront the stuff I didn't want to get into arguments about, so I'm going to follow through."

Harper tossed the wipe into the garbage can and asked, "You want to get into an argument at work? Really?"

Levi pushed his dark hair from his face. "No. I want to get

to a place where we can be in each other's lives. We have to. We work together."

"I would prefer to stay mad," Harper told him as she grabbed another wipe from the pile she'd created and started cleaning the rolling tray she used.

"I don't want you to hate me," Levi told her. The unsteadiness in his voice meant he was serious.

Harper dropped the disinfecting cloth and stared at him. "That would make it easier though, wouldn't it?"

She wondered how long it would take to stop hurting every time they spoke.

"I'll leave you alone if you want me to," Levi told her. "I promise. I will."

There was no hesitation when she shook her head. "I don't want that. If anything, I'm surprised you want to be around me. I'm selfish."

Levi hung his head. "I'm sorry I made you feel that way." He glanced up, his dark eyes meeting hers. "You're working through your shit. I get that. We're just not on the same page anymore and that should be fine."

Harper nodded. "It is fine."

Or at least it would have to be. She couldn't expect Levi to be dragged around behind her, doing only what she needed to do. He deserved so much better than that.

"I'm still sorry," he told her, his voice barely audible over the shop's music. "This sucks."

Harper couldn't agree more. "But, if one good thing came from all this, you called me out on my shit twice."

Levi laughed. "Are you sure that's a good thing?"

For Harper, no, but she couldn't tell him that. Levi had done what he always struggled to do and she couldn't let him backslide.

"Yeah," she told him with a tip of her head.

The corners of his mouth twitched with the hint of a smile.

Harper wanted to go to him, hug him, kiss him, but he wasn't hers and she had to accept that.

A little body ran into the space, arms waving. Instinctively, Harper put up both of her hands and shouted, "Stop."

Eddie stopped so fast his body lurched forward even though his feet had stopped.

"Eddie, you can't be in here right now."

"Noah said I could," Eddie said, puffing out his chest.

Harper let out a long sigh.

"Hey," Levi said to Eddie, "do you want to help me fill the back to school donation bin?"

Eddie's eyes lit up and he nodded furiously. Levi nodded at him and asked him to follow. The two of them disappeared in the direction of the break room where extra donations had been dropped off earlier that day.

Harper stood for a moment watching the space where Levi had stood. She wished he would come back.

"I DON'T WANT TO DO THIS," FRANCES COMPLAINED FOR THE fifth time since they left Silver Sparrow.

Leaving Green Bridge for yoga felt like a betrayal, but when she inquired at her usual studio, they couldn't accommodate Eddie. He was too young and they weren't equipped for that. She couldn't argue, but she promised to keep her membership and continue with her morning classes when the kids were in school. Once the kids moved in with her mom full time, she would still have a spot and the tiny studio wouldn't have lost her monthly payments.

"This is just a trial. I'm not forcing you to go more than once," Harper explained as she pulled open the door to the studio. "You hate it, we don't do it again. Cool?"

The studio was in a condo building. The ground floor had a juice bar, a salon that did lashes and waxing, and the The

Dance Centre. After searching online, The Dance Centre turned out to be the only place in Vale that had mixed-age classes, allowing children as young as five to join. Harper signed them up for a trial and ordered child size yoga mats.

They walked into the low hum and trickling fountains and, somewhere in the distance, flute music. The walls were yellow and sage green. The smell of sandalwood was overpowering for Frances and Eddie, who vocalized their feelings about it. Frances wrinkled her nose and Eddie put his hand over his face.

Harper went to the front desk to check them in. The woman wore a sports bra style shirt with tiny shorts. Frances stared wide eyed.

"It's nice to meet you all," the woman said once Harper gave her details. "Your kids are really cute."

"We are not her kids," Frances said very loudly and very aggressively.

Harper might have been offended if Frances didn't look so uncomfortable by the whole scene. Eddie stared at Harper as if waiting for her big reaction, so she gave him a soft smile for comfort.

"They're my half siblings." She reached up to tap her card to pay for the session. All she could think when the screen of the terminal said 'approved' was how much of a hit her savings account took at that moment.

"Well, that's very nice of you to bring them here," the woman said, as if desperate to find something to end the conversation.

"It's court ordered," Frances went on.

The woman's eyes bulged and shot to the tattoos on Harper's fingers and arms. Assumptions were being made. She didn't move, but Harper could see her debating whether or not she should take a step back. The whole thing made Harper laugh out loud. She had no idea what the woman was thinking, but assumed it was the worst. It amused her.

Harper took the receipt from the counter, thanked the woman, and told Eddie and Frances to start walking.

Harper and Frances found spots at the back of the room, spreading out their mats. Despite telling Eddie to roll his mat out next to them, he went to the front of the room and set his mat next to another boy close in age to him. Harper and Frances watched him as he said hello to the kid and within seconds they were both rolling around on their mats, trying to do some version of stretches.

"How does he do that?" Frances asked. "Making friends is just so easy for him."

"He's little and he's not self conscious like the rest of us," Harper told her as she crossed her legs and folded herself over.

"Yeah right," Frances mumbled.

Harper glanced over and asked, "What's that about?"

"You're not self conscious."

Harper let out a snort of laughter that drew attention in their direction. She sat up. "I'm hyper-aware of myself and all the things I do. Like, I'm wearing a long-sleeve shirt in the middle of summer so that these moms don't spend the whole class making weird faces at me until they get to know me."

Working in her profession, having the friends that she had, she often forgot about the stigma that surrounded body modification. She lived her life like it didn't affect her, but when Harper got dressed that afternoon, she noticed the way Frances stared at her bare arms. She might not care how other people felt about her, but Frances might. Harper grabbed a sweater on the way out.

Frances' eyes wandered around the room.

"No one's going to stare at you. They're just tattoos," Frances said, rolling her eyes.

Harper pulled off her shirt to expose the black cropped tank top. Her stomach wasn't as flat as everyone else's in the room and she knew that, felt that. With Frances being so thin and already dealing with self harm, Harper didn't want to mention that part of her feeling self conscious had to do with her body.

"People are staring," Frances said only a second later. She pulled at the sleeves of her own sweater.

Harper surveyed the people in the room. Frances wasn't wrong. A few women had shifted their gaze in her direction. The teenagers who had joined and a few of the more free-spirited moms didn't seem to care, but some of the people in the room did. There were always a few that had a problem with them and while she often brushed it off, she didn't want Frances to feel like the judgement was projected onto her. She hadn't even wanted to admit that they were related.

Frances stared at her purple yoga mat.

Harper reached for the sweater and pulled it back on, trying to ignore the way it dragged the sweat down her back.

"You don't have to wear it. The sweater, I mean," Frances said in a whisper. "If you're hot."

"You know, if you're hot, you can take yours off. You got a tank top on, right?" Harper asked her. If Frances took the sweater off and she had no scars, no cuts, she would be able to rest easier. But if she didn't...

Frances shook her head. "I don't want to."

A lanky teenager with deep brown skin and intense blue eyes stopped in front of Harper and Frances and asked, "Are you saving this spot?" She pointed to the space next to Frances.

Harper didn't answer, hoping that she wouldn't have to step in.

"Okay," Frances mumbled. "That's fine."

The girl took a seat next to her and waved at a woman who looked like an adult version of herself. The girl turned to Frances and said, "I'm Billie and that's my mom, Natalie."

A friend? Harper hoped this would be the start of a friendship for Frances.

Natalie and Harper gave each other a nod in greeting, but Harper kept her focus on the way Frances avoided eye contact, the way she answered most of Billie's questions without words, but shakes of her head.

"What grade are you going into?" Billie asked.

"Um, nine," Frances answered.

"Me too!" Billie pulled out her phone and said, "Add me."

Frances reached back to get her own phone from her bag, but Harper watched the way she fumbled to retrieve it and took two attempts to swipe away the lock screen. In an attempt to give her space, Harper got up to check on Eddie, making sure he knew to listen to the instructor.

When the instructor announced they were going to begin, Harper went back to her mat and smiled at Billie and her mom, appreciative that Frances had someone to chat with.

As the practice began, Frances sat up a little straighter and kept her eyes focused ahead. The attempt to get the kids out and meet people their own age had worked, but what Frances did with it moving forward, Harper couldn't be sure.

At the front of the room, Eddie had been joined by all the young kids. All four of them were lined up facing forward, mat beside mat. The instructor even took a second to talk to them before getting started. They all giggled and Harper smiled.

Once they got into the heart of the session, Harper eased into her routine. As it was a mixed group, it didn't challenge her the way she liked, but the familiarity, the routine of the sun salutations took her out of her head and into her body through the movements. The tension in her muscles from a long day at work started to loosen. For almost half an hour, she forgot about the drama with her mom, the money she was bleeding from her savings account, how much she missed Levi, and the fact that she was in charge of keeping two children alive.

Harper glanced over to check in on Frances, to make sure

she wasn't loathing the whole experience. That's when she saw it. The t-shirt Frances wore beneath her sweater had slipped out from the waistband of her black joggers. Being in a bent knee version of Downward Dog, her shirt slipped down and exposed over an inch of skin.

The one inch didn't only confirm her suspicion, but it told her she had underestimated the situation altogether. That inch of skin had several large scars, white from healing, but between them a bright red scar, closed but still new.

Feeling overwhelmed by what she saw, Harper fell out of her pose and tried to shake it off. Frances looked at her confused. Harper tried to keep it together, tried not to stare at the evidence, but she failed. Her eyes darted toward it and back within seconds, but the damage was done.

Frances dropped down to her knees and pushed back onto her legs. She grabbed at her shirt, shoving it into the waistband of her pants. Without a word, she jumped up and rushed out of the room. Billie and her mom glanced over, but neither said anything as Harper struggled to her feet.

Trying to keep from disrupting the whole class, Harper darted on tiptoes out of the space. She followed until she was sure Frances only went to the bathroom and didn't make a run for it. In the bathroom of the studio, she would be safe. Harper waited on a bench in the hallway, unsure of what to do next.

CHAPTER TWELVE

THE INTERNET HAD A LOT OF IDEAS OF WHAT HARPER SHOULD DO about Frances. It had been four days since yoga and Frances still hadn't looked her in the eye. Any time Harper opened her mouth, Frances cut her off or left the room, as if terrified of the conversation. The apartment had become even more tense than the week they arrived. All the information Harper collected about Frances came second-hand through Eddie. The only positive, Eddie confirmed Frances was messaging Billie from yoga.

After the horrible yoga experience, Harper removed the painkillers and the sleeping pills she bought when she wanted to stop smoking a joint before bed every night. She didn't know where to put them or what to do. She couldn't afford to throw them out if they would need them again. So as not to make a scene about it, she took them from the medicine cabinet when everyone was asleep and put them in a box in her room. If Frances noticed her removing them, it might have caused the silent treatment to go on longer.

The only break Harper got from the dirty looks and one-word answers came on the Saturday her mom took them. Harper showed up early Sunday morning, earlier than she'd ever voluntarily woken up before, out of fear that without her watchful eye Frances had hurt herself again. She didn't know how much Patricia kept an eye on the kids. How little Patricia had paid attention to Harper at that age made her nervous.

The internet told her to be careful about approaching the subject of self harm and to focus more on the teen's feelings. The blogs and therapy websites told her to expect strong reactions regardless of how well she approached the subject. Harper decided that it meant Eddie would have to be elsewhere when the conversation happened. The apartment was too small to go into the other room without being overheard.

After returning from Patricia and Roger's, Frances came out of the bedroom while Harper typed 'how to talk to teenagers about self harm' into a search bar for the fifth time. Not wanting to have the conversation that minute, Harper closed her laptop and picked up the sketchpad with her client's design.

The design hit close to home since during the consultation, her client said she wanted something that looked textured to hide the self harm scars on her forearm. It wasn't the first or even twentieth time she'd covered scars, though it had a different impact on Harper that time. Harper always hated the idea of 'signs' coming from a higher power, but she couldn't argue with the way certain things kept popping up.

"Can I get you anything?" Harper asked Frances as she put her pencil to the paper, thickening the edge of the butterfly's wing. She hoped she didn't sound as guilty as she felt.

"No."

"Are you hungry?" Harper asked.

Frances didn't answer. Harper twisted around on the couch to see what she was doing. Even while it was happening, it felt like an annoying, overbearing thing to do, but she was on high alert and couldn't stop herself.

Without turning around to confirm, without even taking

her eyes off the refrigerator shelves, she snapped, "Stop being creepy. You're being the worst."

"The worst?" Harper asked, amused. "You think I'm the worst?"

Police sirens, which had been wailing in the distance, passed the apartment. They both fell silent until they faded out.

When the apartment was quiet again, Frances glanced over her shoulder, eyes narrowed. "Well, you're definitely not the best. Just stop staring."

"I'm not allowed to look in your direction?" Harper asked, amused and hoping a little light teasing would get them back into a calmed state.

"Maybe you are the worst," Frances snapped. It wasn't a joking tone. Harper had pushed her too far and made her more angry than annoyed.

"Harper," Eddie called from the bedroom.

She turned back in her seat. "What's up?"

"Come here," Eddie whined.

"You can't come here?" she asked as she set down her sketchbook and pencil.

"Harper," he cried out.

A jolt of panic hit her in the chest. She got to her feet and rushed into the room only a second before Eddie leaned forward and threw up all over his feet. He didn't try to move or even avoid vomiting on himself. Harper covered her nose and mouth with her hand to keep from doing the same thing.

Eddie started to wail as Frances pushed past Harper, then gagged at the sight.

"It's okay," Harper said, trying to put on a brave voice. "I'll handle it."

Harper inched around the puddle of vomit and scooped Eddie up under his arms. She held her breath and carried him out of the room into the bathroom, keeping him out from her body so as not to get his breakfast on her feet. Once in the tub, she turned on warm water and rinsed him down.

He didn't laugh being hosed down in his clothes, instead he kept sobbing, huge cries that left him gasping for air.

"You're going to be okay, buddy," Harper tried to tell him over the wailing. "Sometimes we just eat something that–"

Before she could finish speaking, he went silent. She froze too and, as she feared, he doubled over and threw up into the bathtub. Harper kept her hand on his back, but turned away. Her own stomach ached at the smell and the sound.

She turned off the water and said, "Stay here, just sit on the edge of the tub and don't move. I'm going to clean the floor."

She made sure Eddie sat and was secure before leaving the bathroom. Frances had already moved a bottle of spray cleaner and paper towel into the bedroom, but was perched on the edge of her own bed looking pale.

"It's okay," Harper told her. "I'll clean it up."

Frances leaned a little further forward. "My stomach is hurting too."

"I'm sure it's just the smell. I'm feeling it too. Once I clean it up–"

Frances leapt up from the bed and ran into the bathroom.

Harper realized then that her own stomach ached, and it wasn't in her head.

Despite the body aches, the fever, and constantly running to and from the bathroom, Harper emailed all of her clients for two days, letting them know she wouldn't be able to keep their appointments, but that they would reschedule. She kept the empty waste bins next to the kids' beds empty and made sure that both of the kids had water and plain crackers to nibble on. She ordered a delivery of children's medication for their fevers, but the drivers cancelled twice.

Olive said she couldn't leave work that afternoon, but she would get to the pharmacy as soon as she could.

The kids were suffering, so Harper knew she had no choice. A new layer of discomfort settled into her stomach as she picked up the phone.

"To what do I owe this honour?" her mother asked in the most condescending voice.

"Are you busy today?" Harper asked. She hated the way her illness was so evident in her voice. Her throat was raw from throwing up. It made her sound weak.

"I'm taking the boys to get new hockey gear before the season starts. Should I sign up Eddie now or do you want me to wait until I get *custody*?" Patricia asked.

She didn't say when she and Roger got custody. Something about that detail bothered Harper. While she might be sick and overthinking it, it seemed to Harper that her mother was trying to goad her.

"I don't know if Eddie has any interest in hockey," Harper answered even though it was a struggle. Just saying yes would have been easier than the full statement and she regretted not making that choice.

"Well, find out what he likes, because he needs to be signed up for something," Patricia told him. "The children around here are all into sports or music lessons. He can't just be lounging around the house all day."

Harper tossed an arm over her eyes and rolled onto her back. The sound of her mother's voice added a new layer of suffering to her situation. She mumbled, 'okay' in hopes she would move on.

"I mean it. They're not going to be sitting around, getting in trouble, like you did your whole childhood," Patricia said.

"Oh please," Harper said, finding a burst of energy. "I didn't sit around or get in trouble."

"You got caught selling weed and mushrooms," Patricia scoffed.

"By the school," Harper said. "Not by the police."

"It's disgusting how casually you talk about it," Patricia groaned.

Harper sighed. "I needed new shoes and you told me you wouldn't give me money for some."

Patricia let out a disapproving breath. "Don't try blaming me. You were a delinquent."

"Fuck sakes," Harper whispered to herself. She cleared her throat and said, "I need medication for the kids. We are all sick. They have some stomach thing and they have fevers."

Harper tried not to think about her own fever.

"How are they?" Patricia asked. "Are you making sure they're staying hydrated? Make sure that they get a lot of rest."

"They're hydrated and they're sleeping right now."

"They are just children. You need to make sure they're drinking a lot. A trip to the hospital could complicate things and land them in another foster home before Roger and I even have approval to foster."

Harper hadn't thought of that.

"I'll keep them hydrated." She hated that Patricia talked down to her in that way. Harper had survived taking care of herself during stomach viruses, colds, and flus. She wouldn't let Eddie and Frances suffer alone like she had.

"Dehydration is a real thing. I'll pick up children's Tylenol, but I'm also going to pick up electrolytes and some plain crackers. Oh, those poor kids."

"I have everything but the fever meds."

"It will take me about an hour and a half to get everything and come over. Come to the door. There's no way I'm coming inside if you're all sick. I don't want to risk bringing this home to Roger and the kids."

Her mother hadn't even asked how she was feeling.

Harper knew it was the illness making her emotional, but she still wanted to scream. The virus had weakened her body, but also her defences against her mother.

She hated how much she wanted her mom to ask if she was okay, if she needed anything.

"Hey, Mom," Harper said, "I just got a message from Olive. She said she's on the way over with everything."

Her tone was unconvincing, but she could hear the relieved breath on the other end of the phone.

"That's great. Thank her for me," Patricia said. "Tell Frances and Eddie I'm hoping they get better soon."

Harper told her mom she had to go and ended the call. She tossed her phone into her pillow and squeezed her eyes shut. She didn't ask, not once.

Her phone rang again. Harper grabbed it, wondering if Patricia realized her mistake. Had she called to check on Harper, to make sure she had everything she needed?

Levi's name and a picture of the two of them, cheek to cheek, flashed on her screen. She cleared her throat and answered, "Hello?"

"I still have my key. I'm coming in."

"We're sick," Harper told him.

"I know. Are you decent?"

"Well, I'm dressed, but decent wouldn't be the word I use."

"I'm coming in."

They ended the call. Harper wanted to sit up, to make herself more presentable, but the throbbing in her head and the nausea wouldn't let her. She reached over and grabbed the pack of gum she'd been using to keep her mouth from getting too dry. As she popped two pieces from the packet, the door to the apartment opened.

She didn't need to call out to him, to tell him where she was. Levi came in, mask over his face, with a cloth bag in hand.

"I'm gross," Harper warned him, as if he couldn't see it or smell it even through his mask.

"You look surprisingly decent for the fact that you have been dealing with two sick kids while you are sick yourself." He started pulling things from the bag. "They're passed out, huh?"

"It was a rough night," she told him. "They seem to have stopped throwing up, but their fevers are hanging on."

Levi put two bottles of purple medication on the nightstand and said, "I know you have a stash of Gatorade, but I brought Pedialyte in drink and freezie forms. I also got some lozenges for all your throats. I had some containers of stew and chicken noodle that my mom made when I was up there a couple weeks back. They're in your freezer now for when you guys wanna ease back into eating."

Harper hated how her eyes stung with tears. After how she treated him, after letting him down, Levi still showed up for her in a big way. Her own mother couldn't even ask how she was doing, but Levi came over without even being asked.

It had been a big mistake to let fear take over. She'd been terrified of him leaving and her ending up broken, so she made sure never to rely on him, never to rely on anyone. But he'd left anyway.

All the things she'd been through as a child, all the things she watched her parents and friends' parents do, they stuck with her. They informed all of her decision making. It wasn't like Levi was her dad and he definitely didn't act anything like her mom. Time and time again he proved to be better than they were, but the fear wouldn't loosen its grip on her.

"I owe you," Harper told him, her voice shaking.

"You don't." He reached out and put his hand on hers. "But go to sleep. I gotta get back to work and I really don't wanna catch whatever this is that you got."

Harper laughed and said, "I appreciate it, Levi. A lot."

Levi stared down at her like he might say something else.

Panic rose in her throat, fear he would remind her that the gesture wasn't one of romance, but of friendship. She knew. She didn't need him to say it out loud. That bridge was burned, and she had accepted it.

To her relief, he said, "I'll text you later and see if you need anything else." He took the bottle of water from her nightstand and put it in her hand. "Drink."

With that, he left. Harper rolled onto her stomach and buried her face into her pillow. She didn't want Eddie and Frances to hear her crying.

"Harper," Eddie's little voice said from the bedroom door. Harper wiped her face before she rolled over. She turned around to see that both Frances and Eddie were in the doorway with their pillows under their arms.

It was the first time they were sick without their dad. She hadn't even realized until that moment how lonely they must have felt, sick in their rooms. She tucked up her feet and said, "Climb in."

Eddie climbed in first, tucking himself in behind Harper so his face was shoved into her back. Frances came in next, sliding in behind her brother. She didn't say anything, she didn't even make eye contact, but there was no hesitation. Within seconds, their breathing changed, getting deeper.

Harper was glad that they were able to find an ounce of comfort with her. She was surprised to find she felt the same.

CHAPTER THIRTEEN

"Let me know when you're ready and we can head out," Harper told Eddie and Frances when she arrived at her mom's place the next Sunday morning. Harper had been showing up at Patricia and Roger's at seven-thirty every Sunday and making breakfast for everyone. At first, she did it to make sure her mom felt like she was contributing, but it became more about spending time with Eddie before anyone else got up. He sat at the island with her, talking about all the things they did the day before while she'd been at work.

"Billie and Natalie are going to meet us at the juice bar before we class today," Frances said as she rinsed her breakfast plate and put it in the dishwasher. Eddie stood behind her, waiting to hand off his plate to her.

"Who is Billie?" Patricia asked, narrowing her eyes at Frances. "You're too young to be hanging out with boys."

Frances caught Harper rolling her eyes and turned away to suppress her own laugh.

"Billie is a girl, not that it matters," Harper said with a shake of her head. "Frances hasn't even shared if she's into boys, so calm down."

"I am," Frances said.

Harper looked at her and said, "You're not helping the situation."

Eddie laughed and said in a sing-song voice. "Frances likes boys."

Frances put her hand under the stream of water coming from the tap and flicked her fingers at her brother, getting a few droplets on his face. He squealed, abandoned his plate on the counter, and ran away.

"We're going to pack our bags," Frances said, putting her brother's plate in the dishwasher as well.

Harper nodded at her and said, "I left the new yoga pants in a bag at the bottom of the stairs."

Frances had come to Harper and asked for new clothes to wear to their classes. While surprised, Harper brought up a discount website and they looked for pants that she could feel comfortable in. Frances still wanted to wear her long t-shirts, with a tank top underneath, but it felt like a start. At least she'd ask for the things she needed. It felt like a big step.

Harper hoped that the new clothes would put her in a good mood. After spending way too much time reading therapy blogs and about what parents did in her situation, Harper wanted to talk to Frances about the harm she was inflicting on herself. It had gone on too long without having a conversation. There were a few chances, when Eddie went to bed early, that she could have brought up the situation, but Harper couldn't make herself say a single thing. She was terrified.

She had already taken several steps toward the conversation, like asking both kids how they were feeling about certain things and trying to express her own emotions more clearly. Her search for therapists in her price range, with decent reviews, hadn't been going well, but she hadn't given up. With the start of school approaching, she worried the stress of a new school and no friends would be triggering for

Frances. Harper needed to find a therapist before the start of school.

"Good morning, everyone," Roger said as he walked into the kitchen. He was still wearing his running clothes, damp with sweat. He went to the fridge and poured himself a glass of water.

"I'm glad you're here," Patricia said to Roger. "I wanted to talk to Harper about the first day of school."

Harper got up from the counter and placed her empty coffee cup in the dishwasher before closing the door. The sound of feet shuffling above their heads meant that the boys were playing around and clothes were not being packed.

"What's up?" Harper asked, leaning against the counter. She braced herself for whatever complaint or criticism her mother was about to provide.

"Roger and I should be the ones to take the children to sign up for school on the first day," Patricia said. She folded her arms and stared at Harper. Roger stopped drinking water and waited.

"Thanks, but no thanks. I already filled out the applications for both. It's just as simple as showing all the documentation the social worker gave me." Harper didn't know why she felt so protective over taking the kids to school on the first day. It would be less work if her mother could do it. "Too many people might make the already overwhelming situation worse."

"Well, we are going to be the legal guardians in just a handful of months, don't you think it's right that we're there?"

"In a couple of months, you're going to be pulling them from this school and putting them in another," Harper reminded him. "Can't you have your own first day of school with them then instead of now?"

Patricia's entire body leaned forward as if she were ready to lunge. "So, you're going to miss a day of work for this?

What about money? How are you going to survive without going to work? I know you're not salaried."

Roger put a hand on Patricia's arm and redirected her attention to him. Only then did she stop talking. They seemed to have a silent conversation that no one else could understand.

Harper stared at her mother, not sure what to say. It didn't make sense that Patricia and Roger would come all the way to Green Bridge to be introduced to the schools Eddie and Frances would be staying in for less than half the year.

"Don't worry about where I get my money," Harper told them. "And the school thing, I'm handling it."

"We are going to become their guardians within a few months," Patricia reminded her.

"Yeah, you keep reminding me," Harper said. "And on that topic, I've been meaning to talk to you about that."

"Oh?" Patricia arched a brow, trying to look amused, but there was something else in her eyes. Harper could see a hint of worry in the way her mother pushed a strand of hair behind her ear one and then again.

"What's your plan after? You're going to get guardianship of them and then what?"

Roger straightened like he might have something to say, but he didn't utter a word.

"What do you mean?" Patricia asked. She unfolded her arms and then folded them again.

Harper maintained eye contact with her mother and said, "What are your long-term plans for these children? Are you going to adopt them? Are you going to foster them until they age out? I think they'll have questions about their futures. I definitely do."

"This is something we hope to discuss with the social worker. We're not making any long-term decisions for the children right now."

Roger nodded. "We wanted to discuss this with the children. We decided that it might be best to wait, when we know that we are approved to foster at the very least. We never know what might come up between now and then."

Roger and Patricia looked at each other. Their expressions gave nothing away thought, not from what Harper could tell anyway.

Her mother hadn't thought through what she planned to do with two extra children in the house? She had convinced Harper to pull them out of foster care and for what? If they weren't going to adopt them, they had been shuffled from place to place just to be a foster kid in some other home?

Harper cleared her throat. "I have some legitimate concerns."

At least while they were with her they were with a relative.

"You have concerns?" Patricia raised an eyebrow. She shook her head in disbelief. "Concerns about what? Me being a parent? Harper, I already did this parenting thing with you."

"Concerns about Eddie and Frances' future." Harper started. She took a deep, calming breath and went on. "Not to mention, the last two Sundays I showed up here you were already at work. You agreed to be here for them from Saturday to Sunday. Are you going to do what you did to me and abandon them every time your work calls you in?"

Patricia glanced at the ceiling for several long seconds before she pointed a finger at Harper and said, "I didn't abandon you. I had a job."

Harper thought about mentioning that her mother also spent more time dating than at home, but she caught sight of Roger. He looked pained by the direction the conversation had taken. As much as she wanted to keep going, one of them had to be the bigger person.

Patricia didn't seem to notice. "You've had these children for two and a half months and you're trying to tell me how to be a parent? I raised you just fine. You had a roof over your head. There was food in the fridge, which was a lot more than most of your friends could say. So, don't you tell me I don't know what I'm doing."

Harper wanted to be mature about it, but her mother's comments made her so angry. She snorted out a sarcastic laugh. "Everything I did and everything I became is in spite of you, not because of you. I took care of myself when I was sick. When I got my period for the first time, I had to ask Divinity across the hall to give me money for pads because you weren't home and your boss said you left early that night. You didn't even know I graduated high school."

Patricia pointed a finger at her. "I worked hard to keep you clothed and fed. I won't apologize for that. Everything I did for you and you're still so ungrateful."

Roger put a hand on his wife's arm and whispered, "I don't think this is a healthy expression of how you're feeling. I also don't think it's how you really feel."

Harper heard what Roger said and while she agreed, the anger wouldn't let her back down. "You know what, when you called me to tell me about the kids and Henry, did you know why I thought you were calling? I thought you were calling to wish me a happy birthday, but you never did that, did you?"

"You dropped them off to go out and party the first week they were in your care, but I'm *so* terrible," Patricia said sarcastically. She waved her hands around for effect. "If I'm such a horrible mother, why do you bring them here every Saturday? Just stop bringing them here altogether."

"For real? Are you really saying this?" Harper stared at her. It had been Patricia who told her she needed to take the kids, to pull them out of foster care. All of it happened because for some reason Patricia wanted custody of Frances and Eddie. She decided that she needed to swoop in and rescue them. Did she think that taking his kids would somehow get Henry Wilde's respect from the grave? Did she think they were some second chance to get her life right? It made no sense and Harper allowed herself to be sucked into the middle of what could very well be Patricia's midlife crisis.

Roger put his hands up and said, louder than he'd ever spoken in front of Harper before, "No. We're not doing this. We're not putting innocent children in the middle of this."

"It was a mistake coming here. I just wanted some answers, not a full-blown assault." Harper took a second to steady her voice before she said, "If you still want the kids to stay on Saturdays, I'll drop them off. They like coming here, so I won't ruin that for them, but I won't be coming in anymore. No more breakfasts."

Grabbing her bag from one of the bar stools, Harper stormed down the hallway, trying to calm herself before she went upstairs to call the kids. Frances was standing on the stairs.

"Hey," Harper said, shoving a fake smile on her face. "No rush, but when you guys are ready, just meet me outside, okay?"

Frances stayed still, not saying anything. Harper might have probed further, pushed her to go get ready, but she had to get outside before she screamed or yelled or worse, cried. She grabbed all three of the yoga mats and shut the door behind her.

Across from the front door, on the other side of the cobblestone driveway, there was a small stone bench beneath a massive tree. Harper marched over and threw herself onto it. It had all been going too well between her and her mother. She had to know it would come to a head at some point. She hated that it happened while the children were in the house.

The front door opened and Roger walked out. He had a full water bottle in hand. He sat down on the bench next to her and handed over the bottle.

Her first instinct was to tell him she didn't need the water, but the heat changed her mind. She mumbled a thank you and cracked one of the bottles open.

"Family can be complicated."

"Family?" Harper snorted.

"I know that you and your mother have a strained relationship. I'm not here to push you to fix that." Roger cleared his throat. "I'm not going to speak on that, but I want you to know that I'm here for you and those kids. No matter what happens."

"Why?" Harper asks him. "I still can't figure out why my mom wants to take this on. Like, what is her motivation? She didn't seem to enjoy being a mother, so why is she jumping on the chance to take on the kids of a man who left her?"

"Your mother had good intentions, but I think her motivations are something she needs to discuss with you. They are part of a larger conversation that I cannot share. It's not my story."

It seemed like a cop-out of an answer, but she couldn't imagine Roger would snitch on Patricia.

"Alright, so why are you doing this?"

Roger shifted uncomfortably and said, "Your mother is my family. You're my family."

"Oh." Harper hadn't been expecting that. She hadn't once thought of Roger as family. When she thought about the massive house, the pool, and his two children, she understood why her mother left her old life to start a new one. She always figured her presence would spoil what Patricia tried to build. It never occurred to her that Roger might feel another way.

"We have the means to take on some extra responsibility," Roger explained. "To me, I think it's only fair that you help family if you can. That's always been something important to me."

Harper nodded, still trying to process.

"I can't fix the relationship between you and your mom.

That's something the two of you need to work through, but is there something I can do for you and the kids?" Roger raised his eyebrows, waiting.

"We're good. As my mom said, it's only going to be months before you guys get custody and as long as I can still see them any time I want, I'm not going to stand in the way of that."

He gave Harper's knee a pat before he stood up and said, "Your mother will be glad to hear that you'll be around even when the kids are living here. Maybe this will be what brings you two closer together."

Harper didn't know how to feel about that statement. If anything, being forced to spend time together had made the whole situation worse. They could no longer ignore the things they had spent years shoving down, locking it away so they wouldn't have to confront it.

Roger went on, "The kids need you. You are family."

The front door opened and Eddie and Frances stepped out. Eddie grinned as he bounced down the steps. Frances' expression mirrored what Harper assumed her own face looked like; The corners of her mouth turned down into a hard scowl.

"If you need anything, anything at all," Roger said. He said goodbye and headed back into the house, reminding the kids they were going to the trampoline park the following Saturday.

"You want me to carry your mat?" Harper asked Frances, nodding down at the yoga mats she'd dropped on the cobblestone.

Frances shook her head and said, "No. But can we get out of here?"

Harper stood up, picking up her and Eddie's mats again. "Gladly."

CHAPTER FOURTEEN

"If Patricia catches you with that eyeliner, we're both going to hear about it," Harper called from the living room, where she worked on a sketch for a client between drawing pictures of dogs and cats for Eddie to colour.

The table was full of colouring pages Harper made for Eddie. She'd come to love the simplicity of doing them. Inspired by the raccoons that woke them all up more than a few times, she started working on an entire colouring book with a story, but those she hadn't shared with Eddie yet. She wanted to save the colouring book for a special occasion or for when he needed something good in his life. Harper had a feeling there might be a few rough days ahead, such as the first day of school, or the day Patricia and Roger took custody of the children.

"I hate this," Frances shouted from the bathroom. By the sound of the clanging in the sink, Harper assumed she'd thrown the eyeliner. "I can't do it."

Eddie put his hands over his ears, dropping the pencil crayon onto the table. "Stop yelling. No yelling."

Harper dragged herself up from the couch and said, "She's just expressing her frustration. She's not yelling at you." She mussed up his hair as she sauntered toward the bathroom door.

Frances stood in front of the mirror with her hair pulled into a bun. There were streaks of black all the way out by her ear from wiping the eyeliner away.

"My stupid eyelids get in the way. Why are they like that?" Frances asked, pinching one of her lids. The black tube of liner sat in the bottom of the sink.

"You have hooded eyes. I have them too, so I know your pain." Then it occurred to Harper. "We got it from Henry. I mean, your dad."

Frances glanced away from her reflection and down at her hands.

That's when Harper noticed something on the side of Frances' shirt. Red spotted through the light blue fabric of her shirt. Blood.

Her instincts told her to ignore it, so Harper turned away. She didn't have to deal with it. It wasn't her battle. Frances could take care of herself, right?

Wrong. Those instincts were wrong and she knew it.

Harper spent her childhood hoping someone would notice the signs. She stayed out late and fell asleep in class. None of her teachers spoke up. She got drunk and high while in public places and sometimes right before she showed up to work, but even her bosses said nothing. Harper started leaving messes around the apartment hoping her mother would say anything at all. She never did.

Stepping into the bathroom, Harper closed the door behind her and said, "You're bleeding."

Frances' eyes went wide. There was no confusion about what Harper saw. They both knew exactly what she meant. The panic set in and Frances backed away from her as if trying to find an escape route. Her hands were shaking.

So were Harper's. "Hey, let me help you stop the bleeding."

Frances pulled at the hem of her shirt, turning it so Harper couldn't see. "No, leave me alone. It's fine."

"I can't leave this, Frances. We can't ignore this, okay?" Harper's words came out in a stammer. It embarrassed her that she couldn't hold it together. She dealt with blood every day. Sometimes people passed out and slipped out of the chair in front of her and she took it in stride, catching them or supporting their heads without a second thought. Sometimes they threw up or urinated in their pants. She'd seen it all and didn't think twice about it, yet she could feel Frances' pain. Her own body ached as if she had cut into her own skin.

Harper reached into the basket on the back of the toilet and grabbed a fresh washcloth. She turned on the tap and let the water run. Frances didn't tell her to get out, so she kept going. Once the water was warm enough, she soaked the cloth, added some soap, and handed it to Frances.

"Wash the area and then throw that in the tub." She grabbed another cloth and ran it under the water again. "This one you can use to rinse the soap and toss it into the tub when you're done."

Harper crouched down, still holding the second cloth. She reached into the cupboard under the sink with one hand and pulled out the first aid kit she put together after learning first aid for work.

When she set the bag on the counter, she realized Frances hadn't moved.

"Frankie," she said, using a name she never had before. "I won't look at you right now, okay? Just wash it."

Harper turned around, facing the bathroom door. Her left hand reached back with the damp cloth. She held still, waiting until Frances' fingers brushed hers as she took it.

"I'm going to turn to the sink, but I won't look at you. I want to get out a bandage, okay?"

When Harper didn't get an answer, she shifted only as much as she needed to and opened the kit. Inside were bandages of all sizes, creams and ointments, gloves, tweezers. It was fully stocked.

"Here's a bandage," Harper said, holding one up.

"Um..." Frances swallowed loud enough to be audible. "That's too small."

Those were not words she wanted to hear. Harper reached into the bag and pulled out a large bandage. It was almost three inches long.

Frances let out an exasperated sigh. "Not that long."

Harper grabbed one somewhere in the middle and passed it back. She listened to the sound of it being opened and the slight gasp from Frances as she pressed it on. Harper didn't move, not wanting to make her feel any shame over what she'd done.

"Can I ask what triggered it?"

Frances didn't say anything.

"I know you don't want to talk about it, but we have to," Harper told her. "If you're hurting, we've gotta find a way to fix that."

"I'm fine."

"Come on."

"Seriously, I'm fine. I can deal with it."

Harper wanted to hold her and hug her, but Frances turned away.

"Did someone hurt you? Like before?" Harper asked. She hated how the question sounded. If she was fourteen and someone asked her that, she would have rolled her eyes and told them to mind their own business.

"No," Frances said sharply, as Harper expected.

"If they did, you can tell me."

Frances let out another annoyed sigh. "No one did anything weird to me."

"I thought about hurting myself before," Harper admitted. Saying it out loud made her feel weak, but she realized that Frances might be feeling the same way. "I worked an extra shift to buy a ticket to my high school graduation for my mom. I told her I was graduating and how I couldn't wait to be done, but she didn't show."

Frances said nothing.

Harper had to force the next words out. "It made me feel lonely. Abandoned really. You know?"

Still nothing.

"I realized I told her when it was, but never asked her to come," Harper said.

"You shouldn't have to ask," Frances told her. It came close enough to an admission of her feelings in Harper's opinion.

Harper turned around and met Frances' eyes. She stood with her arms wrapped around herself.

"I'll try to notice so you don't have to ask," Harper told her. "But, I'm new to this, so next time you're feeling shitty, could you try to talk to me?"

Frances didn't speak.

"We've gotta do something, Frances. You can't keep living like this. Do you really want to?"

"I don't know. No."

"Can you let me help you?"

Frances let out a long sigh. "You can't help me. It's my thing."

"I used to think that way too," Harper told her. "But it just gets more lonely."

Frances said nothing, so Harper cleared her throat and went on. "I have friends who think they know me, but they don't know when I'm stressed or lonely or hurt. I deal with that alone and it's exhausting."

Frances glanced down at her feet.

"And there was Levi. I thought I would marry that man one day, but he couldn't be with me, because I wouldn't let him."

"I won't be like that," Frances told her.

"Good," Harper said. "I really hope not."

"But I don't want to talk about this anymore."

"We can take a break for today, but we need to talk about this." Harper braced herself and asked, "Are you going to fight me if I suggest we see a therapist?"

Frances sat down on the edge of the bathtub and shrugged. "Probably."

"Actually, it's not a suggestion. You're going to go to a therapist."

"What if I don't talk to them?" Frances asked.

"Then we'll find another and another, until you feel comfortable talking to one of them," Harper said. "And while we're at it. I'll find myself a therapist and get Eddie one too."

"You should have got into therapy before you covered yourself in tattoos," Frances said.

Harper raised her eyebrows in disbelief.

Frances glanced up and smiled.

"Shit." Harper laughed. "That was totally a joke I would have made, but I thought you were serious."

"I mean, I was a bit." Frances laughed too.

"Okay, fair," Harper said, holding up both hands in a sign of defeat. "I deserve that."

There was a knock on the door.

"What are you doing in there?" Eddie shouted at them.

"So, therapy?" Harper whispered so Eddie couldn't hear.

Frances shrugged. "Fine."

Another little knock came. "Why are you laughing without me?"

Both girls laughed again while Harper reached for the door and let him in.

CHAPTER FIFTEEN

No one close to Harper had ever had a baby before. There were a couple of girls in her high school class that got pregnant and some women she hung around with when partying had children. Noah had kids, but they were already born long before Harper met him. It was different with Maz and Cassidy. Harper stared down at the little bundle of blankets in Maz's arms.

"I can't believe that's your baby," Harper whispered. She couldn't believe that it had been five days since baby Eaton came into the world, according to Maz, screaming and throwing fits. Harper had seen those fists flailing above his head while he let the world know he didn't like being swaddled.

Eddie and Frances sat on either side of Maz, wanting to be as close to the baby as Harper would allow. On the walk from their apartment to the house, Frances reminded her brother that babies don't have defences against illnesses the way they did. Eddie took his job seriously, asking to wash his hands the moment they walked through the door.

"Don't look at me. Cassie did all the work," Maz said with

a chuckle. She winked at her wife, who sat in the worn out recliner.

Cassidy had her feet up and a chilled beanbag that Olive made around her neck. "And that's why you're going to be waking up every night for the next three weeks with him, and not me."

Maz let out a happy sigh. "I'm glad to do it."

Levi and Olive came in with the takeout. Maz had been craving Caribbean food since baby Eaton had been born, but hadn't wanted to leave her wife to make the trip. Cassidy swore they could go without until Maz got up the courage to leave them alone for an hour, but Harper ordered everything she knew they liked. Because she had the kids, Levi and Olive went to pick up the food.

"I'll text Noah to let him know the food is here," Harper said, stepping back from the couch to grab her phone from the bag. Since Maz had planned to take three months off to stay at home with Cassidy and Eaton, Noah had to pick up the slack.

Maz turned her head to look at Harper and said, "While you're texting him, let him know if you would be interested in taking over some of the business side of things."

"What?" Harper asked, confused.

"I was thinking, since you have a few cuties living with you, you might want a little extra money," Maz told her, winking at Eddie. "We thought maybe you'd want to take on some of the admin tasks."

While the idea appealed to Harper, she also didn't want to spend more time away from the kids. They were starting school the next week, and since she worked until six or seven most nights of the week, it would mean she would only see them right before bed. Would they grow up to blame her for not being around during such a crucial time?

It didn't escape Harper that Frances was watching her from where she perched on the edge of the couch.

"The bulk of it is ordering and posting to social media," Maz told her. "And all of it you can do between clients or at home."

Harper arched an eyebrow. "So, no extra hours at the shop?"

"Not unless you want to." Maz shook her head. "And depending on how you feel about the money, maybe you could take a client or two less a week."

No one at the shop lacked the skills necessary to take over those tasks, but Maz would always pick the people who needed it the most.

Harper's face started to heat up at the thought. It was a handout. Maz only gave her the option to take over because she had Frances and Eddie to clothe and feed. Did it mean that Maz assumed she couldn't handle things with the money she already had?

Frances cleared her throat. Her eyes were wide and she gave a quick nod, telling her to do it. Did Frances hope the job would keep Harper busier? They had been getting along, but Harper remembered herself as a teenager. She would have been nice and polite to the adults, if only to keep the peace.

"You'd be the perfect fit for it," Levi said from the kitchen island behind her.

Levi didn't make eye contact when she turned to look at him. They'd been giving each other space. Next to him, Olive's head bobbed up and down.

"There's no one better to cover for me," Maz told her, as if to really drive it home.

Harper could feel she was being duped into taking it. They were using some psychological tricks on her. On principle, she wanted to turn them down. The problem with turning down the job would be turning down the money and the extra time with the kids.

"I'll do it," Harper told them, because she knew it was the right thing to do.

Maz tipped her head back up at her and said, "Good. I'm glad."

"Frances," Eddie said from his spot on the couch, "Did I have this much hair as a baby?"

Harper felt a stabbing pain in the centre of her chest. It was a question that no one in their lives could answer for them. They had lost their history, both mementos and stories. Everyone in the room went quiet, waiting to hear what Frances would say next.

They had no baby pictures. They had no pictures with their father. Would pictures of them still exist somewhere or did they all get thrown in the trash when they were taken into foster care? Did their father's brother still have some? Maybe their mother, wherever she disappeared to, still carried a picture of her children as infants. Harper hoped so.

"You were bald," Frances said, her voice low as if she was aware of how all the adults in the room were trying not to breathe. "And you barely cried."

"Like Eaton?" Eddie asked, eyes wide.

"Oh, he cries a lot," Maz told Eddie in a quiet voice. "He's just on his best behaviour so that you guys will like him."

Eddie craned his neck to get a better view of the baby. "I love him."

Harper wanted to hold Eddie like a baby again. She hated that their father robbed her of the experience. It made her so angry that she hadn't been there for Frances and Eddie as they grew up.

Olive stepped into the space next to Harper and said into her ear, "Take pictures. Lots of them."

Harper pulled the phone from her pocket and moved around the couch, around the table. She crouched low so that baby Eaton's face wouldn't be in the picture since she knew Maz and Cassidy were still deciding on social media rules. She captured a good shot of both kids looking at Eaton before either of them noticed. After that, she had them pose on the couch with Noah and Olive smiling behind them.

Cassidy told Harper to pass over the phone and sent her to stand with the rest of them. Harper slipped onto the couch next to Frances. Olive put a hand on her shoulder as they all smiled for the shot.

"Thanks for offering me the job," Harper said to Maz in the front hallway as she slipped on her shoes. The kids had run outside to look at the community garden that Maz and Cassidy had created where their front lawn once had been.

"Don't get weird about it," Maz warned her. "We take care of each other at Silver Sparrow. Like you and the kids bringing Eaton way too many gifts."

"There's a little care package for the two of you in there too," Harper told her. "Make sure you both take care of yourselves."

"Don't worry," Maz said, "We are really lucky to have a lot of family who want to help. You don't have to worry about us."

Harper shrugged.

Maz held up a hand and said, "Before you go, I have something for the kids." She turned and opened the front closet where all the winter coats and shoes were kept. From a shelf, she grabbed two black backpacks and handed them to Harper.

"Aren't these from the back to school drive?" Harper asked.

Maz nodded. "Yup."

"But they're for kids in the neighbourhood that need them."

Maz raised her eyebrows. "Girl, they are kids in our neighbourhood."

Harper stood still. They needed the backpacks. Between work, yoga, and attempting to keep the apartment clean, she'd been struggling to find the time for back to school shopping. She'd failed and Maz had bailed her out.

"You're going to drown if you don't accept a helping hand," Maz told her. "Take the damn bags."

Harper reached out and took them. "Thank you."

She gave Maz a hug and headed out the door. The kids were looking at the gardens.

Maz and Cassidy found that a house near the bridge that was the border between their neighbourhood and Green Valley. In the couple of years they'd been living there, they had updated the place a lot. They turned the entire front lawn into raised garden beds. A sign stuck in the front said, "Need a veggie, take a veggie."

The houses around Maz and Cassidy's weren't as cute or well kept. Especially the house right next to them, which had been for sale for six months without any offers. The lawn had become overgrown and yellow with neglect. One of the windows had been broken and boarded up. Someone had spray painted a slur on the garage, but Noah and Maz painted over it with leftover paint from their own renovations, making the garage look newer than anything else on the property.

Harper wondered if she would be able to save enough for a down payment on that house. It would take a lot of work and it would mean not taking a trip like she planned, but she could see living next to Maz and Cassidy when thinking about the long term. It would be nice to know she had someone close by. And even though the kids were going to stay with her mom, she wanted a place where they could always come and feel safe.

As she walked past the house, the kids running in front of her, her phone started to ring. Harper glanced at the screen.

Family and Children's Services. She'd been waiting for the call.

"Hello?"

"Hi, Harper, this is Beatriz."

"Thanks for getting back to me." A few drops of rain started to fall. The kids squealed up ahead, amused, not worried about getting wet.

"No problem. I was surprised to hear from both you and your mother on the same day."

Harper's chest tightened. She didn't know why it bothered her that her mother had been in contact with Beatriz, but it felt wrong. Something about it seemed off. Harper swallowed down her panic before answering, "Oh, I didn't know she called. I don't want us to take up too much of your time."

"No problem at all. I'll get in touch with her later this afternoon. I wanted to call you first, check in on Edward and Frances," Beatriz told her.

At least Harper had that. With the children in her care, she could at least get what they needed before her mother started bad-mouthing her to the social worker.

Clearing her throat, Harper said, "Well, thank you. I wanted to discuss something I read in the information package. There was a section that talks about therapy being available to the children."

"Yes, are you interested in signing them up?"

Harper turned toward the doors and windows to make sure no one was listening. "Yes. For both children, eventually, but Frances as soon as possible."

"Is she in crisis?" Beatriz asked.

Regret filled Harper's entire body. She knew she needed to reach out, to get help, but it was so hard. Every life lesson always came back to one thing: Take care of yourself because no one else will take care of you. Harper had learned it the hard way, so hard that she didn't want to deal with another life lesson.

Maz's words came back to her. She didn't want to drown.

"Actively? I don't know. I don't think so. Things seem to be stable for now, but I found out that she's engaging in self harm. It might have been going on for a long time." She barely choked out the words. "I've spoken to her about it and I've told her that therapy is the next step and she agreed. I just need to find her a therapist. I need... well, if you could... I could use some help finding her a therapist that I can afford that can help with this issue and like her dad dying and her mom abandoning her, and like all the foster shit. Sorry, stuff."

Beatriz was quiet for too long and the tension became almost unbearable. Harper's heartbeat picked up so fast she could hear the whooshing in her ears. The rain started to pick up and Frances stopped, lifting her face to it. Eddie watched his sister and did the same. Harper picked up her speed to catch up to them.

"Sorry, I'm messaging someone I think could be a good fit to see if she has availability to take on a new client," Beatriz said. "She does excellent work with teenagers in general, but when I have a teen dealing with the same things Frances is, I prefer if they see her."

Harper let out a long breath. "I hope she has some time."

"How are you doing?" Beatriz asked. "Finding this out must have been a shock."

Harper tried to figure out the right balance. She didn't want to come off too weak, in case the social worker thought she couldn't handle it. Too strong and she would appear apathetic.

"It's a struggle to see her like that. She's hurting." Harper winced. It made her sound too weak. She needed to balance it out. "Hopefully if she sees a therapist, it can get her on the right track toward healing."

"But I'm wondering how *you* are feeling," Beatriz said. "What can I do to support you?"

"I'm good. I'm okay. I'm just worried about Frances,"

Harper told her. She slowed down, despite the rain, to give herself a chance to finish speaking.

"Well, if there's anything I can do for you, don't hesitate to ask." Beatriz said. "Also, I have confirmation. Next Tuesday at three o'clock is available if Frances can take it."

"Yes," Harper blurted out, while tipping her head to shield her phone from the rain. "We'll take it."

Tuesday at three would cut right into the middle of her work day, but she didn't want to put it off any later. She would have to reschedule any conflicting appointments. It felt like it was becoming a regular thing and Harper didn't want to tell Maz and Noah.

When she ended the call, it hit her. She would have to tell her mother about Frances' situation. Her mother would be the one to take over her care. Soon the kids would be living with Patricia and Roger full time and remembering that caused a heaviness in the pit of her stomach. She worried about her mother's reaction and she worried about Frances.

"Harper," Eddie yelled as she approached. "Look at my hair."

He shook his head and some of the wet strands stood up in all directions. Harper shoved her phone in her pocket and said, "Come on. Let's get home before it gets worse out here."

Frances smiled as the rain hit her face and seeing her like that calmed Harper's worries for the moment.

CHAPTER SIXTEEN

"WE CAN'T GO IN?" FRANCES ASKED AS THEY WALKED DOWN THE hallway behind a woman in a white blouse. All the other had children already started their day, but the office needed additional paperwork from Harper, proving she was the temporary guardian. By the time they finished, the national anthem had ended and the hallways were empty.

"We just say goodbye at the door," Harper whispered back. She tightened her grip on the tiny, clammy hand in her grasp. Even though he complained, Harper held Eddie's hand all five blocks to the school.

"It doesn't seem fair," Frances complained.

Harper realized that morning that her own feelings about sending Eddie off to school were shared by Frances. Frances had been nervous all night about the following day, but not for herself starting school. She checked Eddie's backpack twice, made sure Harper added strawberries to his lunch, and picked out his clothes for him. He didn't end up wearing the outfit she decided on, which made the entire morning more chaotic than it needed to be. It didn't take long for Harper to realize Frances wouldn't be getting to school on time and it might have been her plan all along.

"Be grateful you're even walking him to his classroom, you're supposed to be in your own class right now," Harper reminded her.

"I'm happy," Eddie said, glancing up between Harper and Frances.

Harper couldn't figure out why she felt so emotional over Eddie and Frances starting school. By the time she got back from work each day, they would be home. While she might notice it on Mondays and before going into Silver Sparrow while the house was quiet, it felt like something so much bigger, but she couldn't figure out what.

"I know this is another big transition for you guys," Harper said. "You've had so many already, but I think this is a good one."

They passed posters with motivational phrases like 'you never fail until you stop trying' and 'one step at a time' accompanied by pictures of cats. She hoped her statement didn't come off as cheesy as the posters did.

Frances rolled her eyes. Confirmation that Harper had been as cheesy as she feared.

The woman in the white blouse slowed as they came to the end of the hallway. She pointed to the double doors at the end and said, "You can do drop off outside these doors each morning. Edward's teacher, Mr. Carey, will have everyone line up outside when the bell rings and bring them in."

Harper nodded. The woman knocked on the classroom door.

Eddie stared up at her, eyes wide and asked, "Can I go in now?"

Harper had been worried he would fight her when it came to school. She worried he would want to stay home, but he didn't. When she asked him if he planned to make friends at school, he said 'yup' with a smile and total confidence. She couldn't believe he was in such a hurry to leave her.

She couldn't believe how hard it had become to leave him.

The door opened and a man, in his late forties, stepped out into the hallway. He wore a pair of brown trousers and a cardigan with an apple, a piece of paper, and a pencil embroidered into the fabric. He wore a pair of oversized, sky-blue glasses that he had to adjust to look at Eddie. He reached out a hand and Eddie dropped both Harper's and Frances' hands to give it a shake.

"You must be Edward," Mr. Carey said to him.

"Eddie," he said loudly. Harper laughed while Frances told him not to shout inside.

"Well, Eddie, do you want to say goodbye to your people and come meet your classmates?"

"Wait," Harper said, pulling the phone from her pocket. "We need a picture. Please, if that's cool?"

She needed to document all their little moments, especially if they weren't going to be with her for some of them later.

The teacher nodded and smiled while Eddie puffed up his chest and grinned so wide. She thanked the teacher and prepared herself to crouch and give Eddie a hug goodbye. He had no intention of wasting another minute. He waved over his shoulder and took his teacher's hand.

"I love you," Frances called out to him.

Eddie stopped in front of the cubbies that separated the door from the rest of the classroom. "I love you too."

Harper gave him another wave, because one wasn't enough.

"I love you, Harper," Eddie called out.

Harper held her breath for too long. She almost missed the chance to say it back as Eddie started to walk away.

"I love you too, buddy." She blew him a kiss. He did the same in return. When he disappeared behind the wall of cubbies, Harper let out a long, deep sigh.

Frances stared at Harper. "Are you going to cry?"

Harper scrunched up her face and said, "What? No. It was just a cute moment."

It was a cute moment that Harper didn't realize she'd been wanting. It had only been three months with them. It had been a rough couple as well. After everything they'd been through, it never occurred to her that Eddie might say it, but she had been more than a little excited to say it back.

"You can use this door to exit," the woman in the white blouse told them, not realizing the gravity of the moment. Harper knew when she wasn't wanted, so she pushed the door open and held it for Frances to walk through first.

"Look at you," Frances said, eyebrows arched. "Aren't you supposed to be this tough, tattoo person?"

"Who said I'm tough?" Harper asked, bumping into her with her shoulder as they walked off school property. Harper glanced back for a second, wondering if Eddie would pop into one of the classroom windows to wave goodbye. He didn't.

"You wear ripped jeans and crop tops, and have tattoos on your knuckles."

"I have hearts and stars and clouds tattooed on my fingers not 'stay hard' or some shit like that," Harper said with a laugh. "I am not tough."

"But you raised yourself without parents," Frances said.

Harper kept walking, but didn't look at her. "Who told you that?"

"Olive."

"You lost both your parents. I still had my mom." Harper shook her head. "And Olive shouldn't have told you that."

Neither spoke for a while as they walked toward the high school. Harper couldn't imagine why Olive thought it was a good idea to tell Frances that. She had no problem reminding Patricia she'd been absent, but the kids didn't need to know it. They had their own problems to face; They didn't have to be burdened with hers.

"Don't be mad at Olive," Frances said, her voice shaky. "She told us because I was being, like… not nice about having to live with you."

"You were talking shit about me?" Harper asked, arching an eyebrow as a joke.

Frances rolled her eyes.

Taking a more serious tone, Harper followed up with, "I'm not mad at her. I just don't think you guys need to know that. That's for me to deal with, not you."

"I'm glad I know," Frances said.

Harper wondered if she could tell Frances she loved her too. It would be weird for both of them and probably uncomfortable. There was no doubt that her feelings for both of the kids had grown to that of family, despite how little time they'd known each other.

It might shut Frances down if Harper blurted out she loved her too. At fourteen, she'd become more jaded than her little brother. Harper realized it might take time to ease her into those specific words, especially after everything she'd been through.

After another silent stretch, Harper said, "I always wanted a sister, you know?"

Frances tugged at the sleeves of her Silver Sparrow shirt. "Yeah. Me too."

It wasn't 'I love you', but Harper hoped it had the same impact. She had to look away, with tears in her eyes, so Frances wouldn't make fun of her again.

Instead of going out for lunch with Maz, Harper took to the break room with a notepad and a pen. She had a plan and she didn't want to vocalize it until she knew if it was even possible. It also occurred to her that with some hard facts, with some details of all the reasons why it wouldn't work, she would be able to break the spell she was under.

With it all laid out in front of her, the numbers weren't looking great. Housing, food, school supplies, and activities they wanted to do. One income for two kids seemed impossible. She didn't know how single parents all around the city could make it work.

The reality was sinking in as she tapped the numbers into her phone calculator app. The rent alone was killing her. If only she hadn't dipped into her savings for the kids, maybe she could have used it for a down payment on a house instead of the trip.

Harper got up from the table, needing some physical space between the numbers and herself. She pulled out the drawer that housed all the tea offerings that kept expanding. As much as she wanted a chamomile tea to calm her right down, she had a client coming within an hour. She needed to be focused.

"Hey," Levi said, coming into the break room with his lunch in a bag. Maz came in behind him with the last remnants of an iced coffee. They sat down at the same table Harper had left her things on.

Harper thought about going over to flip the notebook upside down, but it would only look more suspicious. Instead, she hoped to distract them with conversation.

"You going up to see your parents next weekend?" Harper asked Levi.

Maz took a sip of her iced coffee before saying, "Oh, you didn't tell her?"

Harper looked between them. "Didn't tell me what?"

"Things are a little uncomfortable right now," Levi said, focusing on his burger.

Maz picked up her phone as if to remove herself from the conversation.

"What happened?"

"I told my parents that they need to work things out with my sister on their own, that I didn't want to get in the middle."

It had been something he wanted to do for a long time, but standing up for himself had never been Levi's forte. Levi did so much for his parents, so much for his family in general. He loved them and knew that they loved him, but their emotions always got the better of them, something that Levi worked hard to keep from happening to him.

Harper never thought he would stand up to them about it.

"You okay?" Harper asked.

Levi glanced up from the burger he was unwrapping. "Yeah. I get that it's the right thing to do, but it sucks."

Maz gave his wrist a squeeze.

Harper gave him a nod. Their situations may have been different, but she understood.

After a bite of food he said, "I wasn't going to say anything, but your eyes keep darting to the notebook. We already saw it."

Maz smirked.

Harper sighed and said, "I hate that you two know me so well." She filled the electric kettle and put it back on the base to boil.

Levi reached into the brown fast food bag and grabbed a fry. "So, we gonna talk about it?"

"If I talk about it with you two before Olive, she'll murder me," Harper told him.

Levi said nothing and continued to munch away on his food. Maz on the other hand said, "I'm not gonna go running to Olive to snitch, so why don't you tell us what's on your mind?"

Harper shook her head. She could deal with it on her own. Right?

Levi glanced up at her. His dark eyes were waiting, almost hopeful that she would say something. She wanted to, she longed to, but she didn't want to put her problems on them.

Maz cleared her throat, set her coffee down, and crossed her arms.

They were there, offering her the space, giving her a chance to reach out. She'd told Frances to reach out if she didn't want to feel alone. She had to offer up the same thing.

If she didn't blurt it all out she might lose her nerve, so she let loose. "I just thought maybe it would be cool if the kids didn't move in with my mom, if they stayed with me. I thought it would be the right move for them and maybe me. Maybe I'm being selfish because I'm attached? Or maybe it's because I'm still trying to show my mom I can handle things? If that's the only reason, that's fucked, but I can't keep thinking it's the right move." She wished the kettle would boil or Levi and Maz would say something to stop her from talking.

"I also think it's the right move," Maz said.

That she expected.

Levi nodded. "Same."

"You do?" She definitely thought Levi would have some reservations about it.

He nodded again.

"But if I did that it would mean that Frances and Eddie would have to grow up in Green Bridge and they wouldn't get to travel or get new clothes whenever they want them or play in sports unless it's free through a charity," Harper explained.

"But you love Green Bridge."

"For me. But they could live with my mom and Roger. They could have a good life there. It feels selfish."

Maz and Levi looked at each other.

Harper opened her mouth to speak, but Maz did first, "Our little girl is growing up."

Harper rolled her eyes.

"You say they'll have a better life, but you're only thinking about money. Financially, yes, Patricia and Roger can give them something you definitely can't. But saying that'll make their life better, there's no way of knowing that."

Harper sighed. "Is this something I actually want or is it me not wanting someone else to help, like everything else in my life?"

Maz clasped her hands to her chest and gave Harper an overexaggerated expression of pride. "So self aware."

Levi raised an eyebrow. "While I appreciate you asking the question, I think you're overthinking it. Why do you want the kids to stay with you?"

"So they don't have to uproot their lives again. There's some stuff with Frances and her mental health that might backslide. And I thought if they stay with me, they can be the focus. I'm sure Roger will treat all the kids the same, I feel like they need the extra attention. Like, is that fair to his kids?" Harper took a breath. "And honestly, I don't know what my mom's intentions are. She's being so weird. Like, these kids are my family, forever. My mom hasn't even said if she plans to adopt them. How can I send them to her when I don't even know what her motives are?"

Maz's face turned serious. "That all seems reasonable."

"And I had this foolish thought that I might be able to buy a house and–"

"What house?" Levi asked.

"The one next to you," Harper said, tipping her head at Maz.

"Yes," Levi and Maz said in unison and then laughed.

Harper tilted her head at them. "With what money?"

Levi shrugged. "Ask your mother."

Harper let out a sarcastic laugh. "Fuck. No."

The kettle started to boil. Harper poured the hot water into her cup with the tea bag.

"Why the hell not?" Maz asked. "It's the solution you need. You get money for a down payment, which will make life cheaper, right?"

Harper scowled.

"Then, you start charging more for your work as an artist, as you should already be doing, and you'll be all set," Levi piled on. He popped another fry in his mouth.

"It's not that easy."

Levi shook his head, disappointed in her answer. "It would be a lot easier if you asked for things you needed."

Maz raised a finger. "Or even just accept the things being offered to you."

Harper wanted to ask if she wasn't already doing that by asking for their input, but then her phone began to vibrate.

Levi grabbed it without looking at the screen and offered it to her. Leaving her tea on the counter, Harper took it and saw the familiar number of Family and Children's Services.

"Hi Beatriz," Harper said when she answered.

"Hello, Harper. The children are in school now?" The pleasantries were gone. The ease they'd talked with before had disappeared. Harper could feel the tension immediately.

"Yes. They're both in school. I'm at work." Then quickly added, "On a break."

"That's great. I'm calling to ask if you might be available next Tuesday for a visit."

"A visit?" Harper asked. "Tuesday isn't great because we have Frances' therapy. Maybe we can book it another time?"

"I can be there after her appointment."

It wasn't a question. Beatriz would be there on Tuesday after Frances' therapy. Harper stared into her tea mug and said, "I guess I don't have a choice, huh?"

"I will see you on Tuesday at four-thirty," Beatriz said

before she ended the call. Harper didn't take her eyes off the mug and the steam rising from it.

"What the hell was that?" Levi asked. His forehead creased in concern.

Maz sat up straight.

They already knew.

"A home visit." Harper turned her gaze to him. "I think someone called Family and Children's Services on me."

CHAPTER SEVENTEEN

Harper bounced her leg up and down as she and Frances sat on the bus, heading back to the apartment. All the plans she had to clean and emotionally prepare for the home visit hadn't happened.

It had been chaotic since Beatriz called to announce the visit. Frances came back from school on Monday frustrated over an assignment she had to do for class, upset that the school was too far ahead of her last one. Eddie had two wet nights in a row after a month without a single accident, causing everyone to be too tired. Eddie's shoes were too tight and he needed new ones immediately. There was no time to clean or buy groceries. Their laundry had started piling up.

When Harper attempted to reschedule her Tuesday client, the client told her if she canceled her appointment for the second time, she would find someone else to do the simple butterfly tattoo. Harper couldn't lose the client or the money. She had no choice but to take the appointment and hope the messy apartment wouldn't be held against her too harshly.

"How did therapy go?" Harper asked, trying to keep her mind off the home visit.

"Can we talk about it later?" Frances asked between sips from her water bottle.

Harper glanced at her with an arched brow. "Promise. You don't have to tell me what you said or anything, but I just want to know how you feel about it all."

"And I'll tell you, but you're being... weird." Frances stared at her. "About Beatriz coming?"

"Yes," Harper said. "I'm sorry. Today should be about you and your appointment."

"My appointment was fine. It was a get to know you thing. I didn't cry," Frances said with a laugh. She reached up and pulled the cord to signal their stop was next. They weren't the only ones that got up and moved toward the exit.

"But still, you went and I'm celebrating that, just maybe after whatever this is," Harper said. She tried not to show her concern, but her emotions were all over the place that day. She feared Frances would be able to read it all over her face. Harper was terrified.

The bus came to a stop. They all filed out onto the street. Harper waved at a woman she once worked with when cleaning The Swashbuckler the first years after high school. The woman waved back before heading off in the direction of her own home.

"She's not going to take us away, is she?" Frances asked when the cluster of people all dispersed toward their own homes. "We're not going back to a foster home, right?"

Harper wanted to answer that question with a 'no', but she didn't know. She had no idea why Beatriz had an interest in doing a home visit out of the blue. Had it happened because she'd been honest about Frances' mental health? Had they assumed she couldn't take care of it?

Because she couldn't answer, Harper reached out to give Frances' hand a brief squeeze. Instead, she clamped her fingers around Harper's. Harper stepped in close to her as words would never give her the reassurance she needed.

They turned the corner onto their block to find Levi strolling out of the house with a garbage bag in one hand. He noticed them, but didn't stop walking. He tossed the black garbage bag into the back of his truck, waved, and drove off before Harper and Frances reached him.

"What the hell?" Frances asked.

"I don't know, but we can worry about that later," Harper said. "Let's try to get in there and tidy up a bit before Beatriz arrives."

As if summoned by the sound of her name, the blue minivan pulled up in front of the house. Harper and Frances stopped walking and waited to greet her. They stood there, still holding hands, for an awkwardly long time while Beatriz climbed out.

They wouldn't even have a chance to make the place presentable. Harper's stomach ached at the thought. Everything that could go wrong had. She really hoped nothing terrible had happened inside with Olive and Eddie.

"Sorry," the social worker said, rushing around the back of the van. Her curls bounced around her face as she came to a stop and sucked in a breath. She had a notebook and pen in her hand. "I couldn't find my pen. Where's Eddie?"

"He's inside with my friend, Olive. We're just getting back from therapy," Harper reminded her.

Beatriz turned to Frances and said, "Do you like Dr. Baillie? If not, you let me know. I can find you someone great."

The version of Frances that had slowly appeared over their months together disappeared. The moody version returned. Her face turned into a scowl, she took her hand back from Harper, and folded her arms across her chest. "Yeah, she's nice."

"Well," Harper said, hoping to move things along. "Why don't we head inside? I know the kids will be getting hungry soon."

"Oh, of course. I'm here to observe, so you can do whatever you guys do and I'll just watch," Beatriz told her with a smile. The smile was so fake Harper couldn't stand it. It hadn't been that way before. Harper liked her, trusted her, but the flags were waving in her face and they were all red.

"Alright then," Harper said.

The three of them walked in silence up to the house. Harper unlocked the main door and then her apartment door, standing back to let them in. Beatriz went first, her head moving as she scanned the place.

Harper followed behind and knew something was different. All the dishes she'd left behind that morning had been cleaned and put away. One of the two bulbs in the light fixture above the kitchen table had been replaced so they both lit up when she switched them on.

Eddie came running around the corner and slammed into Harper as he did every day she got home, and like every other day, she picked him up and gave him a squeeze.

"You've been good for Olive?" Harper asked as she set him back down.

Eddie didn't say anything. His smile disappeared. He stared up at Beatriz, who grinned down at him.

Harper hated that the kids were aware of what her visit meant, of what the repercussions of it could mean. She wished she could reassure them, promise them nothing was going to happen, but she couldn't risk lying to them either.

Olive appeared in the kitchen and said, "Everything was great. We knew you were busy with Frances' appointment today, so Eddie and I read the book he needed to read for homework already."

Eddie looked at Harper. "So, we can read something fun before bed instead."

"I'm going to take a look around," Beatriz said. She didn't wait for an answer and wandered into the apartment.

Harper hated the invasion of privacy, the feeling of having her whole life dissected. She and Olive spent so much of their childhoods making sure everything appeared perfect from the outside to avoid visits exactly like this one.

Unlike every other day, Frances didn't need to be asked to hang up her coat and backpack.

Harper hung up her own things and whispered to Olive, "Why is this place so clean? You're supposed to be using this time to do your homework."

"It wasn't me. It also wasn't me who stocked your fridge and freezer. Like... packed," Olive whispered and then laughed.

Harper jerked the fridge door open. Every inch of space had been filled with fruits, veggies, snacks for kids, and so many kinds of juices.

"Levi?" Harper asked.

Olive leaned in. "The cleaning was Levi. The food was Noah and Cassidy."

Harper couldn't believe they all came over to help her out. She'd known about Beatriz's visit for almost a week and she couldn't even get the house in order. She couldn't even make sure the fridge was stocked. The worst part, her friends knew she couldn't.

"Stop it," Olive said, no longer keeping her voice low. "I can see what you're thinking and that's not it."

"I made my own bed," Eddie said, "And Levi taught me how to tuck the corners."

"And?" Olive asked him with a grin.

Eddie held up his hands, all his fingers splayed out. Harper wanted to pay attention, but she was distracted by the sound of Frances and Eddie's bedroom door opening.

"I know how to multiply by nine," Eddie told her.

That grabbed Harper's attention. "What? How?"

"Levi taught me. Ask me!" His eyebrows danced with excitement.

Olive leaned in, her voice low. "Only up to nine times nine."

Frances didn't stick around to watch. She walked into the living room and watched Beatriz.

"Show Harper what nine times four is," Olive told him.

Eddie, with his hands still up in front of him, counted each finger from left to right until he reached the forth. He put his fourth finger down and then started counting again.

"Three," Eddie said.

"Remember, in tens," Olive prompted him.

Beatriz left the bedroom and headed for the bathroom. Harper had to wonder if anyone closed her underwear drawer. She hadn't.

"Thirty," Eddie said.

Olive nodded. "And the other fingers."

"One, two, three, four, five, SIX." He stretched his hands up closer to Harper. "Thirty-six!"

"Dude," Harper said, "That's really impressive. You can multiply."

"Only by nine," Eddie said with a sigh.

Harper scooped him up and carried him to the living room. "It won't be long before you know how to multiply big and smaller numbers too."

She wanted to tell him that they could work on them together, that she had always been good at math and could help him, but she stopped herself. Depending on what Beatriz found or saw that she didn't like, there was a very real chance she wouldn't be able to help him learn. Her stomach burned with anxiety.

Beatriz came back into the living room where Harper was setting Eddie down on the couch. Frances still stood, arms crossed, glaring. The way that Beatriz's eyes avoided Frances, it was obvious she sensed the glares.

Harper had to bite her bottom lip to keep from laughing. In the first weeks, she'd been on the receiving end of those looks and she hoped it would be a long time before it happened again.

"Would you mind if I speak to the children alone for a few minutes? Just to ask some questions?" Beatriz asked Harper in her fake sweet tone, then she turned to Frances, waiting for an answer.

"You cool with that?" Harper asked Frances. Frances didn't budge, so Harper messed up Eddie's hair and said, "Beatriz is gonna ask you some questions and I'm gonna go sit on the porch with Olive. Alright?"

"Okay," Eddie said, sliding off the couch and onto the floor. From the basket on the lower shelf of the table, he grabbed the new pages Harper had drawn for him, along with the new pencil case.

As they headed out of the apartment, Harper gave Frances' arm a squeeze and said, "Tell the truth and take the mean muggin' down a notch."

Before they were even out of the apartment, Olive started to panic. She waved her hands as if trying to shake off the anxiety. Harper gave her a look, warning her to keep quiet until they were outside. Harper hadn't even shut the front door to the house when Olive started.

"What the heck is going on?" she asked, grabbing Harper's arm. "This isn't 'a visit'. This is a legit home visit, like a take-the-kids-and-put-Frances-in-a-group-home visit."

"Keep your voice down," Harper hissed at her. She pointed at the stairs and gave her best friend a nudge to walk toward them. "And I know. I think it's because I asked them for help with Frances."

They sat down on the steps.

"Help with what?"

Harper sucked in a breath. She didn't know if she should be sharing the details. Or maybe she should have shared them a long time ago. After a long sigh, Harper said, "Frances is self harming. Like, not a few scratches on the wrist kinda thing."

Olive held very still. "Since her dad died?"

"Longer, I think. Like, a lot longer."

"Shit." Olive shoved her hands into the front pouch of her sweater. "I hate that."

"Me too."

"You should have told me. I could have helped."

Harper looked at her and said, "Why would I put that on you? You're already watching them both when I'm working. You stick around when I need you too. You've got your own family shit to deal with."

Olive shook her head. "So what? We're family too. You tell family this stuff and, guess what, if they have the capacity, like I do, they help. You know who else would help? Maz, Cass, and Noah. You know who else would have helped? Levi."

"Fine," Harper said, annoyed. "Then I have something else to tell you."

Olive didn't seem like she believed it.

"I want to take permanent guardianship of the kids," Harper said, "And before you say anything, it's not just to spite my mom."

Olive stayed very still. Either she was processing what Harper said or she was trying to figure out a way to tell Harper she was losing her mind.

Harper didn't like the silence. She had spilled the secret and she was in need of some feedback. "Well come on, spit it out. Do you think it's a good idea or not?"

"Have you told anyone else?"

"I didn't tell Levi and Maz, but they know because they saw me doing some calculations at the Sparrow," Harper admitted.

Another long pause, then Olive turned to Harper and said, "We gotta get you out of this house. Those kids are too different in age to be sharing a bedroom long term."

Harper laughed. "So, you're on board?"

"Obviously," Olive said, "I've been waiting for you to say this."

The door to the house opened. Eddie poked his head out and said, "Your turn."

Frances and Eddie came out onto the porch with their coats and shoes on. Olive gave Harper a worried smile and said, "I'll be here."

The apartment seemed too hot when Harper walked inside. She pushed the sleeves of her sweater up as she kicked off her shoes. Beatriz sat on the couch in the living room, waiting for the conversation. She didn't look up as Harper approached, which didn't feel like a good sign.

Harper lowered herself onto the chair, but stayed close to the edge in case she had to get up and get some space from the situation. She had this intense urge to run out of there.

"I just want to go through a few routine questions," Beatriz said, tapping her notepad as if it were proof that the questions were routine and whatever was happening wasn't targeted.

Harper felt targeted.

She started by asking how much time she spent with the children, what a regular day looked like, what obstacles she'd been facing when it came to the change in her lifestyle. All of those questions felt routine enough. If anything, Harper thought she nailed it. None of it had been easy, but she had really come to enjoy the way her life had been in those months.

Then Beatriz shifted in her seat and pushed a dark curl behind her ear once and then twice. "Have there been any concerns about drugs or alcohol being used around the children?"

There it was, the real reason she had come.

"Nothing more than a single beer with dinner." Harper hadn't noticed until then, but in the months since Frances and Eddie came to stay, she had lost that urge to get drunk with her friends, to get high on a nightly basis. She wished she had time to go out drinking from time to time or hang out in general with her friends, but she didn't have the same desire to get out of control as she had before.

"Have the children been exposed to any illicit drugs?"

"No."

Beatriz sucked in a breath. "Do you regularly consume alcohol?"

"Did my mom call you?"

"Reports come in anonymously."

Her mother had to be behind it. Her breath quickened, her jaw tightened, and a wave of exasperation swept over her. No one in her neighbourhood would call Family and Children's Services on her. Who else could there be? The school? They never expressed any concerns. It had to be Patricia.

"The children saw me drunk one time. I had a few drinks after work. Frances and Eddie were staying with my mom and they were awake when I got there. I assumed they would be sleeping, but Eddie wet the bed that night. It happened right when they got here, the first or second week or whatever. It hasn't happened again." Harper swallowed down the words of anger that pushed up from her chest, ready to scream in frustration. "I wouldn't do that to them."

Her mother's behaviour made no sense. It had been Patricia's idea for her to take the kids. It had been Patricia who pushed when she said it seemed like a bad idea. Why would she do that to her?

"Thank you for answering my questions," Beatriz said. Her face was still void of any emotion. She almost appeared to be a different person from the one who had sat in her office and told Harper what a great experience it would be to have the children for several months.

"Yeah, sure. Anytime," Harper replied, trying to keep from asking her what her problem was.

They both stood.

"Did you draw these?" Beatriz asked, reaching down to touch the colouring pages that Eddie left on the table.

"Yeah, Eddie prefers I draw his pages instead of actual colouring books," Harper explained with a shrug.

"You should create kids' storybooks or colouring books," Beatriz said. "These are great."

Harper nodded, because she didn't know what else to say. She feared that the wrong thing would cause the children to be taken from her care and end up back in the foster system while they waited. The kids didn't need her to mess it up, not any more than she already had.

When they got to the front porch, both Frances and Eddie moved to Harper's side. They positioned their bodies between Harper and Beatriz. The gesture made her smile. She shifted them behind her and together they watched as Beatriz left.

"She's going to take us, isn't she?" Frances asked. Olive looked down at her feet.

Eddie started to cry. Harper scooped him up and stroked his head.

"I don't want to leave," he sobbed, pressing his face into her neck.

Harper cleared her throat, trying to clear the lump that had formed. "I don't know what's going to happen, but I promise you guys I will do everything I can to keep you with me."

CHAPTER EIGHTEEN

"Are you going there now?" Olive asked, her voice getting loud through the phone.

Harper whispered a thank you to the driver and climbed out of the car. She switched the phone from one hand to the other before putting it to her ear again. "I'm there. I'm hoping she's home. She's been dodging my calls for the past two days. I called the hospital and they said she's not in until later."

After dropping Eddie off at school, after confirming no one had called in for an early appointment, Harper called an Uber. The window between the school drop-off and when Maz and Noah would expect her at the shop was small, but she had to get things off her chest before it ruined yet another day.

Olive gasped. "You called the hospital?"

"I never call the hospital. It was one time," Harper said, justifying herself as she stomped up the cobblestone, crunching over a few of the yellow and red leaves that had begun to fall from the trees. Her mother's car was sitting in the driveway. "Oh, she's here. Her car is here."

"Give her hell," Olive said before they ended the call.

Harper knocked on the front door and stood back so Patricia could see her in the doorbell camera. Her mother must not have checked the camera before she opened the door, because she stood up straighter at the sight of Harper.

"What are you doing here?" Patricia asked, stepping back. She was still in her navy blue scrubs, which made Harper wonder if she was coming off a shift or was on her way in. Either way, Harper had no intention of backing down, no matter what her mother's excuse was.

"Did you call Family and Children's Services on me?" Harper asked her, her voice loud and sharp.

Patricia looked around as if they were still in their neighbourhood with neighbours so close that secrets were impossible to keep. In that neighbourhood, no one would hear a simple confrontation, but it had become clear that Patricia didn't want the neighbours knowing her business.

"I don't have time for this nonsense," Patricia said. "I'm heading in for a twelve hour shift and I'm not in the mood."

Harper pointed a finger at her. "Do you know what will happen to them if they get taken away again? Eddie just stopped wetting the bed every other night. Frances self harms. Something like that could push her to more drastic measures."

Patricia put a hand to her chest. "Self harm?"

"If they're forced out of their home and into another foster situation, who knows what that will do to their mental health," Harper shouted at her.

Patricia released the door and shouted back, "Don't act like you have some moral high ground here. A couple months ago, you were partying all week and hanging out with who knows who. You didn't even want to take these kids."

"What do you even care?" Harper threw her hands in the air. "You didn't care before, why do you all of a sudden care what happens to me or what I do?"

"You said you would be coming by Sundays," Patricia

said, shaking her head. "That was your idea and now you're just taking it back."

"You're mad at me for not making breakfast on Saturdays? That's what this is about? All we do it argue, so what's the point anyway?"

Harper turned away so she could look at anything other than her mother's face for a second. She needed to cool down. She needed to get her point across and she could feel herself getting off course. Talking about their relationship, or lack thereof, hadn't been the objective.

Exhaling, Harper turned back to her mother. "So, because I won't make Sunday breakfast, you're willing to risk the getting them throw back into a different foster home? Why would you do this?"

Patricia stared up at the sky. She pressed her lips together as if to let Harper know she had no intention of answering.

Harper ran her hands through her hair and said, "You have no idea what it's like to be dropped into a stranger's home and forced to learn new rules, and know that the person taking you likely just wanted the pay cheque that went along with it. I had six months in foster care and it still stings to this day. You can't even imagine what it would be like for Eddie and Frances to end up back there, for a third time."

Patricia still said nothing.

"I don't know what made you think to do something like this. I don't know how you justify what you did, but I want to let you know that I will do everything I can to make sure they're safe."

Harper had said what she came to say. Knowing that her mother had been the one to call Family and Children's Services, knowing that her mother didn't even think twice about what it would do to them, she couldn't see how their relationship could ever be repaired. All the feelings Harper had about the way her mother treated her paled in comparison to what her mother had done to those children.

"You were getting too attached," Patricia said finally. Her words were soft, hardly audible over the breeze that shook the changing leaves.

Harper raised an eyebrow. "Excuse me."

Patricia straightened her shoulders as if feeling renewed confidence. She stared straight at Harper and said, "You were getting too attached to those children. In a few months they will be moving in with us. They need to be here."

Harper let out a loud, sarcastic laugh. "You know what, mother, you're right. I am attached. They're my family and if you think that I'm just going to give them up to you without a fight, you're wrong."

Patricia folded her arms. "You can't keep them."

"I'm going to try."

"I'll stop you," Patricia shouted at her. There was panic in her voice.

"I figured you would try."

Patricia stepped back into the house, like she was going to slam the door, but then she came back out. Her eyes were wide and her mouth opened and shut, like she was trying to stop herself from speaking, but couldn't. She pointed a finger at Harper and hissed, "You can't do it. You can't take them. You can't just take those kids and disappear out of our lives."

"What? Disappear?"

"Yes! You'll just go off and I won't see you or those children."

"I didn't disappear. I haven't even left the neighbourhood. You're the one that left," Harper shouted at her. Had her mother forgotten how fast she packed up her things and moved in with Roger when that ring was on her finger?

Did Patricia really think she was going to do the same thing that both of her parents did to her?

Patricia's face changed from twisted in hurt and confusion

back to a hardened expression. "I will do everything in my power to make sure those kids come here. I will not let you take those kids and take them from our lives, you hear me? I won't allow it."

"I don't even know what you're talking about. Like, do you even know me at all?"

Patricia turned around and stormed back into the house. Before Harper could call her out, she slammed the door hard behind her.

Harper shook her head. It made her so angry that her mother could fight so hard for a pair of kids that weren't even hers. Having custody of them was more important than building a relationship with her daughter.

Spinning on her heel, she marched down the driveway. By the time she made it to the street, tears rolled down her cheeks. Her mother wanted to ruin Harper's chances with the kids. She wanted them all for herself. The same mother who couldn't even remember her own daughter's birthday laid claim to the children of the man who had abandoned her. Both of Harper's parents wanted those children, yet neither of them had ever wanted her.

CHAPTER NINETEEN

The high arms of the waiting room chairs got in her way, but Harper hunched over the sketchbook trying to draw the scene that afternoon from memory. She showed up at the edge of school property, keeping her distance while Frances finished talking to her friends. Under the autumn leaves of a massive maple, Frances tossed her head back as she laughed. It had been such a moving scene, and Harper wanted to document it. The entire bus ride to the therapist's office, she replayed the moment in her head so she would be able to get it right, so as not to forget even the smallest detail.

A woman walked into the office and told the receptionist that she was there for her appointment. She almost sat in the seat next to Harper, but at the sight of her, the woman clutched her purse and moved across the way. Harper could feel the woman staring at her. If she wasn't on a mission to get as much out of her head and on paper as possible, she might have smiled and tried to speak to her to watch her squirm. Instead, she kept her head down and used her pinkie finger to smudge in a shadow that the tree cast across the ground. She would have to revisit the drawing and work on the details of the background and the other people in the picture, but the drawing version of Frances had come together better than she'd expected. She'd come to know that face well, so much so that drawing her and Eddie from memory had become something she did quite often.

Harper's phone vibrated. She flipped the cover of her sketchbook down and fished into her bag until she found the source of the vibration. The message was from Olive, who had taken Eddie to the animal shelter only a few blocks from the therapist's office so he could see dogs. As she double tapped on the message to open it, Harper wondered if Olive had picked a spot for them all to go to dinner when the appointment ended.

> You'll never guess whose account I found.

As she opened the link, Harper wondered if Levi had rejoined social media for a personal account. Right away, she knew that was not the case. The account's profile picture was faceless, a picture of a hand putting up a peace sign. The name at the top said FWphoto with a few underscores, but how many, she didn't know. It had to be Frances' account.

The images on the profile were all black and white. The most recent photograph didn't have the face of the child in it, but Harper knew it was Eddie. He stood on his tiptoes peering out the window of their bedroom, through the bars on the windows. There was another of him from the back as well, standing at the edge of Patricia and Roger's pool with floaties on his arms.

Then Harper noticed a picture of herself. She was curled up on the love seat, sketchbook on her lap. The composition of the photograph was decent. Much better than she expected from a fourteen-year-old. The light coming from the side table lamp cast half of Harper's face in a glow. The picture was flattering, even though Harper's hair fell into her face and her nose wrinkled up in concentration.

The best part of the picture, something that Frances didn't likely know, Harper had been working on a sketch of Frances and Eddie. Eddie colouring at the table. Frances on her phone. It took her almost a week to finish, but that night, the night Frances took the photo, she'd started it.

Harper almost closed the app, so she wouldn't get caught if Frances came out, but noticed the caption below.

The sister.

Harper closed the phone, but couldn't control the smile that spread across her face.

Less than a minute later, Frances came out of the office, wiping her face with a tissue. Her cheeks were blotchy and her eyes swollen.

Harper stood up and rushed over. "Is everything okay?"

Frances nodded, but didn't meet Harper's eyes.

Her therapist gave a sympathetic smile and nodded. "I would describe it as a good session, but a tough one. Do you think so, Frances?"

"That sounds about right," Frances said, keeping her eyes cast downward.

Harper mouthed her thank you to the therapist and said, "See you next week."

While they put on their coats, Harper asked, "Do you wanna go look at puppies with Eddie or take some time to walk around first?"

"Walk first."

"There's this park on the way to the shelter," Harper mentioned, leaving out the fact that her and her friends got drunk there one night after trying to get into a strip club while they were only eighteen. "Now that all the leaves are changing, it would make a cool spot for some pictures."

Frances looked at her for the first time. She gave Harper the 'you're being weird face', which she had perfected with a single raised eyebrow and pursed lips. "Olive showed you my Instagram, didn't she?"

Harper laughed, holding the office door open for her to leave. "How did you know?"

"She followed my account, like, right before the appointment. I knew she wouldn't be able to keep her mouth shut."

"The photographs are great. You're talented. Your dad would have been proud," Harper told her. Their voices seemed loud in the empty hallway, even though they were keeping them low.

"Proud? I doubt that."

Harper touched her arm and said, "No, seriously. Your dad really wanted me to like photography as much as he did. He wanted a kid who understood his passion. God, I hated it, but I went along with it because I wanted him to like me."

It took all her willpower not to say how it hadn't worked. She'd let him down.

"He didn't do photography around us," Frances said.

"I might have ruined that for you." Harper sighed. "I annoyed him with how bad I was at it. When I took to drawing, like my mom used to, it was obvious I really let him down."

She held open the exit and let Frances walk through first. The autumn air had cooled over the past week. The forecast didn't call for snow, but it didn't feel like it would be long before it came.

"Are you angry that he left you?" Frances asked as they started down the sidewalk.

"I thought I was over it, but I've been angry lately," Harper said honestly. "Finding out about you and Eddie. It kinda complicated my feelings, added new layers to the whole thing, if that makes sense."

Frances glanced down again.

"But that's not on you. My anger isn't at you." She paused, because she didn't know how to put into words how the whole thing made her feel. It had gotten so complicated, so fast. "Finding out about you and Eddie, finding out I had siblings, that hurt for a couple reasons. Being left behind sucks, but–"

Harper hadn't finished speaking, but Frances asked, "You were mad at him for having other kids?"

"Are you sure after a tough session you wanna talk about this?" Harper asked. "I don't mind telling you, but if it's too much, we can discuss it later."

Frances shook her head as they stopped at a light to cross the street. "No, I wanna know."

Harper sucked in a deep breath. "I was mad at him for leaving me and knowing that you got to have him in your life, that made me jealous. I wished I had that."

Frances wrapped her arms around herself. The light turned green and the walk sign appeared.

"But there's something else," Harper told her. She hoped she got the words right and hoped that Frances wouldn't become overwhelmed by what she had to say. She cleared her throat. "Henry took away the chance for me to be in your lives all these years. And if this really tragic thing hadn't happened, if your dad hadn't died, I still wouldn't know you. That makes me angry too. That's why it's so hard."

Frances didn't speak.

"It makes it complicated and I'm angry at him for making it complicated, making it harder for us." Harper tried to clear things up, making sure Frances knew it wasn't her fault, not at all. All she could do was hope she hadn't made things worse.

Frances looked up at Harper and said, "Sometimes I'm mad at him for dying. But sometimes I'm mad at myself because I forget to be sad."

Harper wrapped an arm around Frances' shoulders and pulled her into her side. "I don't think mourning someone's death is as straightforward as being sad until you're not."

"That's what my therapist said too," Frances told her.

"Well, that's two wise people telling you," Harper said with a light laugh, "So, don't be so hard on yourself."

Frances rolled her eyes and said, "I'll try."

"Sorry I don't talk about Henry much," Harper said. "I didn't know what to say, but I should give you the space to talk about him more."

Frances shook her head. "Not if it makes you upset."

Harper stopped her at the trailhead to the park and faced her. "He's your dad. Talk about him as much as you want. I can handle it."

"Can you? Can you handle it?" Frances asked.

For a brief second, Harper thought she was serious, but then Frances smirked. Harper gave her a 'pffft' before they started walking again.

After a few seconds of quiet between them, Harper asked, "You okay though?"

Frances nodded. "Yeah, I'm good."

It seemed like a good time to tell Frances that she wanted to apply for permanent custody, to ask her how she felt about it. She thought about how discussing it without Eddie around might be the best way. At least at first.

Then she thought about Beatriz coming for the home visit and what that might mean. Had she been there just to gather information for Patricia to use in court should Harper ask for custody? She couldn't get Frances' hopes up, not until she knew for sure.

AFTER GIVING EDDIE A BATH AND GETTING HIM BUNDLED UP ON the couch so Frances could read him a story, Harper went to find a specific box. She sat on the floor of her bedroom, having pushed a pile of clothes out of the way. It had to be there, somewhere shoved at the back of her closet.

She pulled out the plastic bins of art supplies, the ones

that once filled the room the children were in. At one time, the thought of giving up her studio room made her feel like she was losing a part of herself. When Levi suggested he keep a few things in her studio, the proposition offended her. She couldn't believe he had the audacity to even ask such a thing. Did he not realize how sacred the space was to her?

It seemed like such a ridiculous thing to be protective over. It was just a room, a room that had more than enough space for Levi's things. The apartment had space for another person. It could have been four of them. She could have been dealing with everything with a partner, but she messed that up.

At the back of the closet, the box she'd been looking for. In black marker it said 'stupid shit'. She dragged it out and slid back across the floor for space. The cardboard of the box no longer felt structurally sound. One of the flaps tore as she popped it open. It had a musty smell of years of being shoved in the back of cupboards. Harper hadn't opened it since packing it back when she was ten.

At the top of the box were a few shirts that her mother almost tossed in the garbage when she first realized Henry had left. They were shirts of his favourite bands; Nirvana, The Red Hot Chili Peppers, and Radiohead. They were too big for either of the kids, but she would keep them safe for them, should they want them later. There was a stuffed bear that Henry bought Harper for her fifth birthday. It had been one of the few times he'd gone out of his way to get her a gift on his own. Patricia hadn't been the one to pick it out or wrap it. Even as a child, Harper knew because he walked into the apartment and tossed it in her direction, no wrapping paper, not even a bag.

What was beneath the bear was what she'd been looking for. In a brown leather bag, the camera kept pristine for all those years. Henry had purchased it with one additional lens from the local pawn shop.

Harper took the camera out of the bag and held it up to her eye. She remembered the way Henry sighed when she held the camera with hands on either side of the frame, instead of with one beneath the lens. He didn't care that it was too hard for her little hands.

There was an envelope at the bottom of the box that Harper didn't remember putting there. She set the camera back into the bag and placed it on her bed. She lifted the envelope out of the box. There were no markings on it, but the weight and feel told her there were photographs inside.

There were a lot of photographs. Baby Harper with Patricia. Baby Harper with Henry. Some of the pictures of Henry and Patricia alone. They were so young, not even in their twenties yet when the photographs were taken. Neither of them were smiling in any of the photographs.

Her mother looked the same, but in the pictures, she had a slightly thinner frame and her eyebrows seemed to sit a little higher when she was young.

Harper wondered if Henry had aged well, but that thought was fleeting. When the kids first arrived, she noticed how they had their father's cute, narrow nose and his pouty lips, but it took time to realize they also had his eyes, not just in colour, but also round with puffy eyelids.

Getting to her feet, Harper grabbed the pictures, the camera, and the stuffed animal. She walked into the living room where the kids were still reading the book. She sat down next to Eddie's feet and said, "I've got some things to show you guys."

"Is that for me?" Eddie asked, pointing at the bear.

Harper handed it over. "Your dad bought him when I was young. I thought you should have it."

Eddie stuck a hand out from beneath the covers and grabbed the bear. He pressed it to his chest and said, "Thank you!"

"And Frances, I wanted you to have this," Harper said,

passing over the camera. "It takes film, so we'll have to get some. I can probably show you the basics, but if you want to get into a class or two, we can always figure that out."

Frances took the camera out of the bag and ran her fingers over the silver and black body. She picked up the second lens from the bag and held it in her hand. "It's heavier than it looks."

Harper held onto the pictures, debating whether or not to share them. They had lost all the pictures they had with their parents and any family she might not have known about. They had no one to reach out to for copies. All details of their past had been taken from them. Sharing her memories, the physical, concrete ones, felt out of touch.

But at the same time, they should have a picture of their dad.

"What are those?" Eddie asked, reaching for the pictures.

Harper didn't react fast enough. She couldn't hide them away now. It would only make things more confusing for the kids. Harper took a photo and handed it to Frances and then gave another to Eddie. They were pictures of Henry, wearing band t-shirts and flannels, looking smug. Patricia must have taken the pictures. Maybe Harper had during their lessons. She couldn't remember.

"I know you guys don't have any of your old pictures or things like that, so I thought you might want to keep these," Harper suggested. She took the three pictures of herself with Henry and set them upside down on the table. She figured she might want to look at them some day.

"Thanks," Frances said, but her face was in a scowl.

"You look a lot like him," Harper told them. She reached out and tapped the tip of Eddie's nose. "I can see you in the pictures of him."

"Really?" Eddie asked, studying the picture, squinting to see what she saw.

"Like what?" Frances asked.

The answer came easy. "The colour of your hair, your nose, your chin, your eyes."

Frances touched her hair. "Yeah?"

"Definitely."

Frances glanced up and said, "I thought you looked a lot like him. Like, even before the pictures."

Harper's breath caught in her throat. "Oh, yeah?"

"Yeah," Eddie said, "you look like dad and Frances."

Harper wondered how that could be true. Frances and Eddie had such perfect faces that told the world that they were siblings. No one could mistake them for something other than brother and sister.

"Yeah, you got that Wilde DNA," Frances said with a laugh. "Powerful stuff, I guess."

Eddie crawled across the couch and leaned against Harper. "You're a Wilde like us."

CHAPTER TWENTY

The thought of picnics made Harper's skin crawl. She didn't want to sit in the dirt and eat off paper plates. She's done enough of that out of necessity as a kid after losing their first apartment. Her and her mother would find a place in a park to eat when they had been cooped up in the car too long. They would look like any other family having a picnic, but Harper hated the whole scenario, especially the cold instant oatmeal and the non-stop sandwiches.

Not only had Eddie asked for a picnic, but he asked for ham and cheese sandwiches. The thought made Harper queasy. She would do it for him.

Since Beatriz's visit, things between the three of them were fragile. The lack of knowing put them on edge. Every time Harper's phone rang, they all went still. To calm everyone's nerves, Harper started mentioning the name displayed before answering, so they would know it wasn't Social Services coming to take them away. Tensions were high, so when Eddie asked for a picnic, Harper couldn't say no.

Even though the temperature started to decline into autumn, they packed two throw blankets from the couch and all the fruit they could find. Harper and her mom could never afford grapes, so she made sure to pack red and green grapes. Between the three of them they wouldn't be able to eat them all.

The park was in Green Valley. It was small and there were houses on three of the four sides, but trees had been planted in an attempt to shield them, to make them feel like they were really in nature. Harper spread out one of the two throws on the ground and flinched at the thought of trying to scrub grass stains out.

"Billie lives near here," Frances said as she spread out the second throw.

"Oh, it's around here?" Harper pretended she didn't check the rideshare app both times Frances asked to go to Billie's place. It might have been the first time Frances shared something with Harper freely, and she didn't want to ruin it by saying 'yeah, I know'.

Eddie had abandoned them for the climbing structure the second they arrived. He waved from the top and Harper waved back.

"Did you want to invite Billie to come hang out?" Harper asked her. She's brought sketch books to keep herself busy if the kids decided they didn't want to hang around her.

They both sat down on the blankets facing Eddie.

"Nah. Eddie wanted a picnic with us," Frances said.

"He's going to make a friend in less than five minutes and forget all about us," Harper reminded her. It didn't seem to matter where they took him. Coffee shops, yoga classes, the grocery store, Eddie said hello to everyone.

Frances didn't say anything, but continued to watch her brother. A small girl with pigtails on top of her head stopped playing to watch him.

"If you want to invite Billie over to our place some time, Eddie and I can get out of your hair a bit. I know it's not cool with us hanging around." Harper laughed. She knew it probably embarrassed Frances to have Harper as her guardian. Then it occurred to Harper that Billie's mom might have a problem with her daughter hanging out in Green Bridge. "Unless it's the neighbourhood that…" The rest of her sentence died in the air.

"It's not that," Frances said. "I'm not, like, ashamed or anything."

"It's okay if you are. I used to be too."

"I'm not. At least your living room just has a painting of naked people. Dad's living room was full of things he took out of the stolen cars, things he thought we could use." Frances stared up at the cloudy sky. "He couldn't stop taking their stuff."

Harper let out a sigh. "I didn't know he was bringing his work home with him."

Frances shrugged. "I didn't know about all of it. I didn't know he was selling cars to, like, organized crime guys or whatever until the lady, Cathy, at our last foster placement told her husband in front of me. Dad hid that stuff from us. Eddie just assumed people gave him stuff. I figured he stole it, but I didn't know it all."

"He didn't bring people by, did he?" Harped asked. "Like, sketchy people?"

Frances tipped her head in Harper's direction and stared up at Harper with a look of disbelief. "No. He didn't bring anyone. I don't know if he even had friends."

"Did you get to go to his funeral?" Harper asked. While Frances continued to talk openly, Harper would keep asking more. "I don't really know what happened to you both in those first weeks."

Frances nodded. "Greg and Cathy took us. No one talked to us. Grandma brought his ashes. They wouldn't let us touch it. And there were a couple people we didn't know, and our uncle."

"Christ. You actually saw Harry?" Harper shuddered at the thought. "I didn't know he was out of jail."

"Just for the day. He had an escort." Frances shivered like a cold breeze crossed her path. "He's creepy."

Harper turned and said, "He's so creepy. Henry always kept him away from me."

"Us too. The only other time I met him, he showed up at our apartment asking dad for money. Dad didn't even let him in."

A long sigh escaped Harper and she took those few seconds to compose herself, to not go on a rant about how sketchy Harry was.

Frances looked at Harper, her face serious, and said, "Dad wasn't around a lot, so I don't know what his social life was like."

"I'm sorry to hear that," Harper said, feeling a heaviness in the pit of her stomach. It hurt her to know that they had to live that way.

"He didn't want to be a dad. Especially when my mom left. He checked out."

It never occurred to Harper that she and Frances had lived similar lives with different parents. The struggles Harper went through with her own parents were mirror images of how Frances and Eddie had been forced to live.

She reached out to touch Frances' hand, knowing that no words she said would be enough.

Frances snatched her hand away and said, "Don't pity me or whatever."

"I'm not pitying you," Harper told her. Then with an arched brow, she said, "I was trying to comfort you though."

Frances stared at her, looking poised to argue. Her face softened after a second. "Oh, okay."

"That day that we went to the mall with Olive, when you first got here, Olive told me that you and I had a lot in common," Harper said. "I told her I doubted it. I think she was right though."

Frances gave a quiet chuckle. "When I'm your age, I don't have to tattoo myself and buy only black and moody clothes, do I?"

Harper stuck her tongue out at her. "Nah, you express yourself and deal with your shit anyway you want to." She caught herself. "As long as it's healthy, safe emoting."

"You're ruining it," Frances told her, deadpan.

Harper smiled. Eddie came running from the climbing structure and shouted, "I'm hungry." By the time he reached them, his cheeks were pink either from playing too hard or the cool air. He kicked off his shoes, sending one to the left and one over Harper's head, then he jumped onto the blankets.

"What are you doing?" Harper asked, scrambling across the grass to grab the stray shoe.

"I want a sandwich," he said, "And juice box."

"Say please," Frances told him.

He tipped his head toward the sky and shouted, "Please."

They ate their sandwiches and a lot of grapes. Harper made Eddie sit with them for fifteen minutes after eating, worried he would make himself sick if he got up and started running around so soon after. She had no idea about the rules of eating and playing. She would have to look it up when she got back to the apartment.

When Eddie darted off again, waving at a little girl he called 'friend', Harper said to Frances, "I'm sorry that both of your parents were shit. But I'm also sorry you lost your dad."

"I'm sorry both of your parents were shit," Frances repeated. "And I'm sorry you lost your dad too."

Harper didn't feel like she'd lost anything. The fact that her father had picked another family over hers didn't have a grip on her anymore. He'd messed up and he emotionally scarred his kids; Harper wouldn't forgive him for that, but she didn't care about that old version of family. Sitting there with Frances, waving at Eddie on the top of the slide, that was all the family she needed.

She hoped no one would come in and take them away.

CHAPTER TWENTY-ONE

The phone call came while Harper was deep in focus on her client's tattoo. She found the right position that gave her the least discomfort, the best lighting, and allowed her to stretch the skin with ease. When Maz stuck her head into the room to let her know she had a call, Harper didn't answer. Her focus was on the tattoo and she couldn't wait to see it finished.

Seeing her design of a fox in a pasture come to life made her feel like she accomplished something. Each time she finished a tattoo, she felt like all the things she couldn't do didn't matter. She did good work. She was good at her job. From start to finish, she gave someone what they wanted and when they walked out of the shop, they took her creation with them.

"Harps," Maz shouted over the hum of the tattoo machine and the music playing through the studio. "Take a break. You're needed on the phone."

Harper might have suggested she take a message, but her thoughts went immediately to the kids. Had Eddie gotten hurt at school? Had Frances hurt herself? After apologizing to her client and suggesting a break to get food, Harper tossed her gloves in the trash and headed out to the front desk.

Maz picked up the phone again and said, "Thanks for waiting. Let me pass you over to Harper." After handing over the wireless landline, Maz patted her on the back and turned down the music by a few decibels.

"Hello?"

"Harper, it's Beatriz."

Her throat and mouth became dry. Her grip on the phone tightened. It had to be the phone call she'd been dreading. Had she called to say that they were taking the kids? Would they get shipped off to some stranger to start all over?

"What's wrong?" Harper asked.

"I'm sorry to call you at work. I attempted your cellphone, but we're in a slight time crunch. There's been a change to the schedule and I would like your permission to move forward."

"The schedule?" Harper stumbled away from the desk and sat down on the couches in the waiting area. She pressed the phone against her ear and asked, "What do you mean?"

"As Patricia and Roger have been approved for foster care and are petitioning for permanent guardianship, we need to set a date for the hearing to determine custody," Beatriz explained.

"They've been approved?" Harper asked. It was fast, too fast. It had only been five months. Five months was not enough time with the kids.

There was a pause on the other end of the line. "Yes, last week. I thought they would have mentioned it by now."

"That's okay. It's sooner than expected, but at least we're not dragging it out anymore. Right?" Harper's hands were shaking.

"Yes. I was able to secure a date for a custody hearing on November 28th."

"A month."

"Yes," Beatriz said. "Just over a month."

It didn't feel like enough time to get all the details figured out. Despite looking every day, she hadn't found a three-bedroom apartment that she could afford in the long term. No judge was going to allow the kids to stay in a home where they couldn't have their own room, especially when Patricia and Roger could offer not only their own rooms, but a pool, and a better school district.

Harper could sense the social worker had more to say. "This is a lot to take in."

"Sometimes, even when we prepare for the inevitable, it still takes us by surprise."

"I want to apply for custody," Harper said.

There was silence on the other end of the line. Harper wondered what it meant. Was it concern, relief, confusion? Harper assumed concern.

"No matter what, the kids don't lose, right?" Harper said, hoping Beatriz would see it that way. Harper or Patricia. The kids wouldn't be back in foster care.

"Thank you for letting me know. I will make sure this is correctly documented," Beatriz told her. "I will send an email with additional information in the coming days."

"Thank you," Harper said, trying hard to keep her composure.

They ended the call and Harper headed for the break room. She was glad her client had offered to get lunch. She needed a minute to collect herself.

Only moments after she shut it, the break room door opened again. She turned to find Levi standing there instead.

"What happened?"

Harper pulled her shoulders up to her ears for a second and said, "The custody hearing is November 28th and I'm not ready."

"They would be doing those kids a disservice if they didn't give you custody," Levi told her.

Harper sat down on the edge of the couch. "Remind me

why this is a good idea. Remind me that I'm not ruining these kids' lives by fighting to keep them from my mother and Roger."

Levi sat down next to her. "You're building a life for those kids the way my parents did for me, Harper. You're building a space of love and understanding that they need," he told her. "Maybe you don't see it, but I can. You have pictures of them in your station and you check your phone for messages from them every time you can. When you think about your day or week, they are at the forefront of your plans. You put them first."

"You make me sound like a saint. I'm not a saint."

Levi chuckled. "I definitely wouldn't say you're a saint and things still might be messy and hard as you go forward, but you've done a lot in a short period of time."

"Thanks for saying that," Harper said.

"I got you." He took her hand in his.

She missed that.

"Can I ask a favour?" Harper asked him, giving his fingers a squeeze.

"Of course. What can I do to help?"

"I know your sister isn't practicing family law in the province, but do you think she has any connections in the area?"

Without hesitation, Levi pulled out his phone. "Let's find out."

CHAPTER TWENTY-TWO

On Sunday morning, Harper showed up at Roger and Patricia's house and rang the doorbell. It had become the new routine when picking up the children. It didn't matter what the weather, she waited on the porch while they gathered their things.

Roger opened the door and said, "Hey, I texted Frances to come back. She's at Izumi's house."

Harper slipped her hands back up into the sleeves of her coat to keep them warm. The early November temperatures dropped below seasonal. The sun set earlier and earlier every night, yet the days felt so long.

"Your mom is having a soak in the tub. Why don't you come in? Frances should be here any minute." Roger kept his voice low even though Harper doubted Patricia would be able to hear a single thing from the second floor.

"Alright," Harper said. "Is Eddie almost ready?" She left her coat on, but took off her shoes.

"He's already packed. They're just in Kayden's room playing video games. I'll call him down in a minute. Give us a second to talk." Roger waved at her to follow him into the kitchen, so she did.

"Oh, here," Harper said, pulling out some printed photographs. "They're copies of some pictures I took on Halloween. Eddie was a dog and Frances was a forest witch. She almost didn't dress up."

Harper didn't know what was going to happen, what would be decided about the kids' future, but she wanted to make sure that they wouldn't lose themselves again. They had lost pictures of themselves, of their father. Harper didn't want that for them again. If they went to live with Roger and Patricia or if they stayed with her, she would never keep all their photographs in one place. They wouldn't stay locked away on her phone. She wanted them to have tokens to remember the good times.

Roger took the photographs and smiled. "Did you make the costumes? They look unique and great."

"That was Cassidy. She's got that skill, not me. That's her standing next to them." Harper pointed at Cassidy standing next to Maz. Maz held baby Eaton, dressed as a vampire bat, in the group shot. Olive had crouched in front, arm around Eddie and a big smile on her face. Harper and Levi were standing behind the kids, his arm was around her waist like old times. She had printed a copy for herself, too.

Roger stuck the pictures to the fridge with magnets.

Harper cleared her throat. "So, Frances' making friends on this side of town too, huh? Apparently, she struggled with friends at her last school, but it looks like that's behind her."

"A stable environment can really help with that. Gives kids self esteem, you know?" Roger told her. He gestured to the coffee pot. "Would you like a cup?"

She shook her head.

Harper wondered if his comment about a stable environment would be the lead into talking about how they'd received approval to foster, how they planned on taking the kids as soon as possible.

Roger leaned on the counter and said, "You've done a

really amazing job with the kids over these past couple months. I have to admit, I was worried."

Harper gave a throaty chuckle. "You weren't the only one. I was pretty certain it would end in disaster."

"I should clarify, I knew you could handle it. I had no doubt you could do it, if you wanted to, but the wanting to was the part I worried about. It's a big job, raising children."

It had never been her intention to make people think she didn't care. She hadn't been given the time to process before she was expected to make a decision. All the information had come at her along with the expectation that she would help, no questions asked. Harper had never been great at doing what she was told to do.

"They told me Frances and Eddie would get split up if I didn't take them. Because they planned on sending Frances to a group home." Harper picked at the skin around her nails.

There was a creak on the floor over their heads. Harper listened for her mom coming down the stairs, but no other sound came. She didn't want to be there when Patricia came down. The tension hadn't subsided. Their text messages were limited to factual messages about the kids. Nothing more.

Harper wanted to get the words out before Patricia appeared or Frances came back. "At first, all I could think about was how my whole life would change. For the first time in my life, I have money coming in and my own place, and when they told me about the kids, I knew how big a job it would be. Plus, I'd just been dumped."

Roger nodded at her to go on.

"It freaked me out that my social life would be out the window, for sure. I'll admit, I really didn't want to take on the responsibility. No more travelling. No more partying. No more dating. It all seemed like an inconvenience."

Roger's phone vibrated from the kitchen counter where it was charging. After raising his pointer finger, asking for a moment, he grabbed his phone and started typing out a message.

There was more creaking. That time, it sounded like it came from the edge of the hallway. Harper pushed her chair back and walked toward the entrance to the kitchen. There didn't seem to be anyone there. The front door was shut. No one was on the stairs.

"Okay, sorry," Roger said, returning to the kitchen island. "Go on."

"So, all those things I worried I wouldn't be able to do, turns out it wasn't that big of a deal. I'm not too stressed about leaving that life behind. Except maybe travelling. I would like to travel. I would like to do guest spots at tattoo shops around the world and just see other places."

"You still could, even with the kids. It would be harder with the three of you and you would have to make compromises, but those things are still possible as a parent or a guardian," Roger told her. "Of course, if you have the money."

Harper appreciated that Roger understood, despite being well-off, not everyone had the means to live like he did. He didn't have blind optimism that things would work out for everyone, since not everyone had the same circumstances as he did.

"Your mother and I were going to wait until tomorrow to tell you, but I assume you already know our foster application was approved," Roger said.

Harper stared into her glass. "Yup."

"How are you feeling about that?"

"Conflicted, which is basically how I've felt about everything since my birthday," Harper admitted. "It's good to know you guys can be there for them if I can't, but..." She didn't think 'over my dead body' would be the most appropriate way to tell Roger that she would be fighting them for custody. He'd approached the whole situation with kindness, so he deserved the same in return.

Instead, she tried, "I have to fight for custody of them. I want custody of them."

Roger didn't argue with her. He seemed to be expecting her to say exactly that. He leaned on the counter toward her and said, "I know growing up you didn't have it easy. Even with your mom. She talks about that time a lot."

Harper looked at him, unsure of where the conversation was going. She didn't know if he really understood the Patricia that she grew up with. Roger and his kids, they got the version of Patricia that Harper wanted. Roger had been a witness to their arguments, but did he know?

Harper cleared her throat. "I'm not sure we would both have the same outlook on how things unfolded."

Roger said, "Your mother has expressed a lot of regret about the way things have played out, both when you were a child, but also recently."

Over the years, Harper learned people expected her to forgive and forget. Her mother had made some tough choices, wrong choices, but she was only human, they said. Harper didn't know if she could handle hearing that from Roger too.

Roger went on. "Your mother and I have had some disagreements about the way things have played out in our home."

That took her by surprise. Despite his job, Roger didn't seem to like confrontation in his home. It never occurred to Harper that he would pull her aside when it was only the two of them.

"While I understand that your mom was young and she made terrible decisions because she wasn't given what she needed growing up, I understand your side of things as well. I can't even imagine what it must have been like for you to see your father involved with Frances and Eddie after leaving you behind. And then your mother offered to take them.

After being left on your own so much as a child, that must have been devastating."

A lump formed in her throat as she listened to him. She couldn't believe he could understand it from her point of view.

"You're not just saying that to get me to say something that shows I'm unfit or unstable, are you?" Harper asked with a laugh.

Roger stood up straight and said, "No. I'm not."

"Because I'm not going to give up trying to get custody of them. I want to fight for them and they deserve that too," she told him. Harper hated that the tears came. As much as she tried to blink them away, they were too powerful to stop.

Roger grabbed a box of issues from a cupboard and handed them to her.

The front door opened; Frances came into the house with the dramatics of a teenager. She announced her return and dropped her coat on the stairs. Harper used the few seconds of Frances' production to get her tears under control. She tucked the tissue into her sleeve so the kids wouldn't see.

Frances walked into the kitchen, looked between Roger and Harper and said, "Can we leave? I want to go now."

CHAPTER TWENTY-THREE

Telling the children about the custody hearing had been on Harper's mind since Beatriz called a few days before Halloween. Her plan had been to do it after she picked them up from Patricia and Roger's on that Sunday, but Frances' mood and attitude gave Harper pause.

Instead of worrying about the court date, Harper worried about Frances' mental health. She'd retreated into herself again, like the days when she first came to stay with her. Things had been going so well, but had fallen off. Harper worried what that meant and what might happen.

As much as she wanted to push off telling her for yet another day, she had an appointment with the family lawyer, thanks to Levi's sister, the next morning. The date of the hearing had come up on them fast and she couldn't leave them out of the loop any longer.

"Frankie," Harper called out to Frances, "Could you come into the living room for a couple minutes?"

"No."

Harper had searched the internet looking for ways to talk to kids about being in a custody battle with two people who aren't your parents. The searches came up with ways to reassure your children in a divorce. Harper had to take what she could from them.

"Then can Eddie and I come to you?" Harper called back. Eddie glanced up from the television, finally cluing in that a conversation had been happening around him.

"No."

"It's one or the other. Pick one," Harper told her, getting ready to get to her feet.

A huge sigh sounded from the bedroom, along with the sound of feet shuffling along the floor.

Out of worry over Frances' mental health, Harper found reasons to keep the bedroom door open, to check in on Frances from time to time. She even offered to do laundry well before a full load, looking for signs of any blood.

"What do you want?" Frances grumbled from the door that separated their bedroom from the living room.

"Can you come sit?"

"Do I have to?"

"Yes."

"*God*. Fine." She scuffed her feet all the way across the living room and tossed herself onto the couch. She bumped Eddie in the process, who whined at her to stop touching him.

"What's going on?" Harper asked. "What's got you upset?"

As if to let everyone in the room know her feelings, Frances grabbed a couch cushion and screamed into it. When she brought it down from her face, she asked, "Is this really why you dragged me all the way out here?"

"Did something happen?"

Frances glared. "No. I'm just sick of you always being in my business and I'm sick of sharing a room and I'm sick of the fact that I can't even go out when it gets dark out because this neighbourhood is so sketchy."

"And you have somewhere you want to go at night?"

Harper asked her, trying to keep her cool. The truth was, she felt defensive about the things Frances said. They were things Harper had been trying to fix, with the exception of being in her business. Harper had no intention of stopping that.

"That's an annoying thing to say," Frances said.

"Listen, I think I've been really cool with the amount of attitude you've given me this week. You have every right to feel what you feel, but you can't treat people like that. There will have to be some consequences."

Frances raised an eyebrow. "Like what?"

"Like not going to Billie's on Friday night."

Frances said nothing. She turned to stare at the back of the couch, which meant Harper had picked the right punishment. She hoped it wouldn't come to that, but at least it was in her back pocket if necessary.

"Is that why you dragged me out here?" Frances asked, mumbling.

Harper cleared her throat. "No. I wanted to talk to you about the upcoming hearing. It's only a couple weeks away now."

Frances sat up and wrapped her arms around herself.

"What hearing?" Eddie asked.

"Remember how Beatriz said that after a while a judge would have to make the decision of where you guys lived? Remember how Patricia and Roger said they would like you to come live with them?"

"Would we have our own room?" Eddie asked.

Harper swallowed hard. "I'm sure they would let you keep the room you already have there. I don't see why not."

Frances didn't move. She didn't look at Harper.

"Do we have to move?" Eddie asked.

Harper hated that she needed to have that conversation.

"It's not decided yet. The judge needs to listen to everyone's information and make a decision about what they think is best for you both. What's going to be the best place for you to become the awesome people you are." Harper reached over and gave Eddie a tickle, hoping it would be enough to keep him from worrying, from being scared.

She wouldn't be able to do that for Frances. Frances understood the seriousness of the situation. Her blank stare spoke volumes.

Harper would have to keep a closer eye on her.

"And again we don't get a say in anything," Frances mumbled.

"You get to have your input. They want to know what you think, where you wanna go. They take that all into consideration," Harper told them.

"But if they say we have to stay here with you, then we have no choice?" Frances asked.

That sentence hurt Harper far more than anything else that Frances said to her in the past. All the rude remarks, all the jabs about her dad not wanting her, none of them compared. The pain in her chest made it hard to breathe.

The words hurt the most because Harper had actually thought things between them were going well. She'd foolishly thought that Frances wanted to stay with her, not because they were family by blood but because they had grown to understand each other.

Apparently Harper didn't understand Frances at all.

It took her almost a full minute to collect herself. Frances glared at her the entire time, making it harder to control her racing thoughts. As much as it hurt her to say it, all Harper could do was reassure Frances.

"I will tell the judge that I will respect your wishes, whatever they are. I believe you're old enough to make that decision for yourself," Harper told her.

Eddie shed the blanket he was wrapped in and climbed from the couch onto Harper's chair. He tucked himself against her chest and said, "I want to stay here."

Harper kissed the top of his head, but didn't say anything.

She worried what false hope would do to them, how it could damage them if they didn't stay.

Frances climbed up from the couch and said, "Am I excused now? Are we done with this annoying heart to heart?"

Harper couldn't be sure that her voice would be strong enough to answer her, so she nodded. Eddie didn't move and Harper was glad about it. He seemed to need her comfort and she definitely needed his.

CHAPTER TWENTY-FOUR

Harper sat at the front of the shop with inventory that Levi had laid out that afternoon to be put away. He spent the morning picking out the pieces he wanted on display before his clients came in. With two walk-ins filling up his lunch hour, he didn't get a chance to put them away.

Harper organized everything by colour, putting them into the glass cases in a rainbow, switching out the stuff that hadn't been moving. She hoped to be done before he finished up with his last client, but she could hear his throaty chuckle as he walked to the front of the store. He paused his conversation about aftercare for a brief second and Harper assumed it was then that he noticed her. She had another couple minutes before he came over to tell her she didn't need to be putting away his stock. It would give her enough time to put the overstock away.

"Hey," Levi's voice came from next to her after he said goodbye to his client. He crouched down to where she was sitting on the stool and said, "You don't need to do that."

She glanced up and shrugged. "I had time between clients, so I thought I might as well get it done."

"Well, I appreciate it," he said. He didn't get up. He

braced himself on the window ledge and went on, "I just wanted to make sure that the lawyer Teyah got you in touch with was helping."

"He's been great and I think he admires your sister a lot. He might even have a crush on her," Harper told him with a chuckle. "But thanks for setting that up. He's taking us on pro bono, and while I could probably have done most of it myself, he's handling the paperwork."

"Really?"

"We've got a lot of the paperwork in order already. He said that it isn't likely to be an easy battle, but we have genetics on our side. Apparently that means something."

"Are you feeling good about it?" Levi asked.

Harper shook her head. "Not really. Patricia and Roger have too many resources and we already have a few strikes against us. The visit from Family and Children's Services, the neighbourhood, the fact that the kids don't have their own rooms." Harper swallowed hard, trying to push down the panic. "The tiniest slip up and the judge won't care if we share DNA."

Levi nodded and said, "I'm glad you're taking the professional help."

Harper stopped stacking the plastic boxes and asked, "Am I really that stubborn that you think I wouldn't use a *professional*?"

Levi shrugged, his face scrunching up. "Well…"

Harper rolled her eyes. "Alright, fine. But, yeah, he's been great."

Levi smirked and stood up. "On that note, I'm going to pick up something to eat. Do you want me to grab you something? My treat."

"Sure," Harper said with a smile. "You know what I like."

"Yeah," Levi said, his voice quiet. "Yeah, I do. I'll be back in a bit."

Before he could move, Noah came up to the front of the

shop, grabbing the wheels of his chair hard and fast. Harper stopped what she was doing and Levi stood back, but didn't leave.

"Grab your shit. Go home," Noah said to her. "Olive just called."

Olive wouldn't call if it weren't an emergency. Harper couldn't think of one thing that Olive couldn't handle on her own.

Harper didn't hesitate. She pushed the box back and got to her feet.

"All she said is that it's Frances and it's fucked," Noah told her.

Harper reached down to grab the box she'd emptied and Noah swatted her hand away. "Leave that shit and go."

"I'll drive you," Levi said. "Grab your stuff and I'll get the truck started."

Harper rushed into the break room and grabbed her things. Her heart raced with all the things it could be. Her mind went to the worst.

Frances had promised Harper that her self harming didn't mean she was suicidal, but immediately she worried that the stress of the hearing and things being tense in the house had pushed her depression to a new level.

Levi had pulled the truck up to the front of the shop. Maz called out to Harper that she would finish wiping down her station and to call if she needed anything. Harper didn't absorb a single word at the time, but she waved while running out the front door.

Harper and Levi didn't talk on the few blocks to her house. Even though the speedometer showed he sped above the limit, her leg bounced, wishing he would go faster.

He drove his truck right up onto the sidewalk and told her to go while he parked. Harper didn't wait until he put it in park before she leapt out and ran to the door. Eddie stood there, his face pale and his eyes red with tears.

"Come on, buddy, come inside, okay?" Harper ushered him through the front door, to keep him off the street. When she turned to see Levi climbing out of the truck's cab, she left Eddie and rushed inside.

Olive stood in the middle of the living room, her hands clasped to her chest and her chin quivering. "She won't let me in, but something bad's happened. I'm sorry, Harper."

Harper rushed around the couch and grabbed Olive by the shoulders. "Bathroom?"

Olive nodded.

"Let me in," Harper shouted, banging on the bathroom door. She hated that the bathroom door had a lock. With children in the house, what was she thinking? Why hadn't she removed the lock?

"Don't be mad," Frances said, her voice way too calm. "Please, don't be mad."

Harper sucked in a deep breath. Even though she yelled, even though she banged on the door, she wasn't angry. It was fear, and she hoped Frances would understand that.

Hearing Frances' voice gave her a split second of relief. It didn't last, but Harper tried to calm herself, tried to sound like she wasn't upset.

"I'm not mad," Harper promised her, "But I am really worried about you. Can you let me in?"

The sound of the lock releasing caused a new level of panic to rise in Harper's throat. She had been nervous about being locked out of the bathroom, but as the door opened she realized she had no clue what she'd walk into.

What she found made her head spin. She closed the door behind her and used it to keep herself on her feet. Frances sat on the edge of the bathtub in her underwear, her black tights around her ankles. Blood ran from the outer side of her thigh all the way down to the fabric. Both of Frances' hands were clasped over her leg. There were drips of blood on the tiles toward the door.

"Fuck, Frances, what happened?" Harper tried to breathe through the wave of nausea that hit her. Sweat collected on the back of her neck and down her back. It became hard to catch her breath.

"It was too deep," Frances said. "I cut too deep. Not on purpose. I didn't even realize. I was just so mad."

Her face was stoic. There were no tears. The muscles in her face were oddly relaxed. Even when she looked at the river of crimson streaming down her leg, she didn't flinch.

"Can I look at it?" Harper asked, even though she didn't want to. Before Frances answered, she reached into the built-in shelf and grabbed the first aid kit. It had never occurred to her how often she would have to use it.

Outside the bathroom there were voices. Levi and Olive talking. Eddie shouting to be let into the bathroom. Frances didn't seem to hear them. She sat very still, barely blinking. It unsettled Harper.

It would have been easier if Frances was hysterical, Harper thought.

Harper ignored the blood running down Frances' leg and went straight for the wound. It was then she noticed the scars. They ran from her knee up to the band of her underwear. From what Harper spotted before, she had cuts running up to her ribs as well. She'd known it was bad, but that extreme had been out of the realm of possibility. Her mind never would have made up a scenario that would be that drastic.

"I need you to move your hand," Harper told her. "I need to see what we're working with."

"No," Frances said.

"I can't help unless I can see it."

"You can't help."

Harper was pretty sure she was right about that. "I have first aid training. I can try."

Frances made eye contact with Harper and then started to cry. "I didn't mean to. I've just been so mad at you."

Her instinct was to defend herself, but she pushed past it. "Can you tell me what I did to make you angry?"

She shook her head.

"I promise I won't be upset by anything you say. If I made you mad, I want to know so we can fix it." And Harper meant it. Anything she'd done that caused that pain, she would take full responsibility for. She couldn't let it happen again.

Frances took a few gasping breaths to steady herself and said, "I heard you saying you can't travel and you can't have fun and we use your money or whatever. You said taking us... you said we were an inconvenience."

"I didn't say that," Harper said, confused.

"You did. At Roger and Patricia's. I came in and I heard you, so I left and came back in." Every word was punctuated with sobs or desperate breaths.

Harper set the cloth on Frances' knee and took her face in both hands. "You're right. I did say that I couldn't travel and that I was using my money, but those were just my initial reactions, before I even met you. Right after that, I said how none of those things matter now. Now I look forward to hanging out with you and Eddie. That's basically all that I want to do."

"You're just saying that," Frances cried.

Harper shook her head. "No, that's the truth. When we get out of this bathroom, you can ask Roger, okay?"

Between body-shaking sobs, Frances said, "But you're sending us to live with them, with Patricia and Roger."

Harper used her thumbs to wipe tears away. "Frances, I'm not sending you away. I got a lawyer because I'm trying to keep you with me. It might be out of our hands, but whatever happens, I love you and Eddie. I'm not going to disappear even if some judge gives Patricia custody, alright? You're my family. We're the Wilde siblings. You're stuck with me, kid, whether you like it or not."

Frances let out a cry and then folded forward, leaning her

head on Harper's shoulder. Harper wrapped her arms around her little sister and said, "Frances, I want to talk about this more, but right this second, I need to look at this. It's still bleeding."

They both sat up. Harper grabbed the warm, wet cloth and said, "On the count of three. You count down, okay?"

"Okay." Frances' voice shook. "One. Two. Three."

"Levi," Harper shouted as she clamped the cloth over Frances' thigh. "You're gonna have to drive us to the hospital."

CHAPTER TWENTY-FIVE

Sitting up all night made Harper's entire body ache, but she wouldn't have it any other way. The nurses offered to cover for her while she went home to pick up some things, but she wouldn't hear of it. She needed to be there for Frances, no matter what.

Despite Frances' objections, Roger paid for a private room. The window next to her bed overlooked the back of the hospital, away from the roads and parking lots. There was a view of a forest off in the distance and expansive, snow-covered lawn in the foreground. Despite Harper's insistence that she should take a look, Frances never glanced out the window.

The sun filled the room, but Frances slept on. Harper hadn't been able to sleep, even after hours of sitting in the emergency room. Once they stitched her up, once the social workers were called, they still had to wait for a room. A psychiatric hold. Frances had been so angry until they gave her a sedative to help her stop crying.

Harper wished someone had given her a sedative too.

Patricia and Roger eventually took Eddie back to their place for the night. Harper couldn't believe that her mother left without a fight, without a snarky comment. Any drama between them had been set aside for Frances. They were united and if they'd had a moment, Harper might have thanked her mother.

A woman in blue scrubs came into the room carrying a tray of food. She said nothing, placing it on the table at the foot of the bed, then left. Harper got up and gave Frances' shoulder a squeeze.

"I want to leave," Frances said, her voice groggy as she sat up in bed. The mattress, pillow, and sheets all crinkled beneath her.

"Maybe this afternoon. But that will depend on a few things." Harper wondered if maybe she should have sugar-coated it, but it wasn't her style. Frances needed to hear the truth anyway.

"The bleeding has stopped."

Harper sat up straight in the plastic chair and stared at her. "You know that's not why you're here." The psychiatrist told her as much the previous evening.

"You had to agree to this." Frances didn't even sound accusatory, which was more unsettling. She opened the lid on her food, closed it again and pushed it away.

"I did agree to this. Even if I didn't, even if your social worker didn't, your doctor would have." Harper hated to admit it. She didn't want to make things worse, but lying about it wouldn't make it better either. The whole situation had spiralled out of control.

Harper's entire life, she'd made sure everything was in check. She could handle everything that was thrown her way. There had been a plan, but that plan went to hell when she got the call about Henry, about the kids. All the safeguards she put in place crumbled. Turns out that she couldn't handle anything if she hadn't planned for it. Harper couldn't believe how useless she became in a crisis.

"It's not fair," Frances groaned, resting her head against the white, crunchy pillow. "I'm fine. It's not a big deal."

Harper swallowed. "It is a huge deal, Frances. I'm sorry I didn't do more. I should have talked about your dad more or been more confrontational about your cutting. I should have told you that I wasn't going to leave you."

"It might happen anyway," Frances said. "That's the way it goes. Whether people like it or not, they leave."

Harper swallowed the lump in her throat. How could she argue with that? She'd spent her whole life feeling that way. Taking a deep breath before continuing, Harper said, "We can't really control those things. I couldn't control my parents leaving. No matter how clean I kept the apartment or how happy I was to see my mom when she came home, she still looked for reasons to be anywhere else."

"Dad left you," Frances said.

Harper nodded. "He did."

"And he left us."

"He didn't want to leave you."

"He was gone all the time, like Patricia did to you. He always had better things to do." Frances' voice was raised. She narrowed her eyes at Harper. "And you don't even know him. He didn't care."

Harper raised her eyebrows, but said nothing. It didn't hurt the way Frances wanted it to. Henry Wilde, if he'd stayed, would have caused a different kind of heartbreak, the kind Frances faced. She couldn't change the way the past played out and she no longer wanted that to dictate her future. All Harper wanted to do was move forward, move forward with the kids, with her friends, with her family.

Frances' shoulders relaxed as the anger subsided. "Sorry."

"It's cool. You get a pass."

Frances smiled, but then rolled her eyes.

"Is it possible that Henry was trying to make money to

support you guys? You told me he kept the dangerous side of his work away from you guys. It kinda sounds like he cared."

Frances dropped her gaze to the blue hospital blanket. "Maybe."

"You're still allowed to be mad at him though," Harper said. "That's a normal feeling. Got it?"

Frances didn't look up, but nodded. "Got it."

"Just don't let it consume you, okay? Talk to me or talk to your therapist."

Frances looked away. "I'm gonna try."

Harper sighed. "Good. Now, eat."

Frances took the lid off her plate. Eggs, bacon, and fruit. Frances pushed the eggs to the side, but started to pick at the rest.

While she ate, Harper tried to come up with a game plan. They would increase her therapy. They would get her into some support group. Maybe they needed to move out of Green Bridge or get her away from the city altogether. She'd been through her mother abandoning her, her father dying, and being forced into foster homes all within the city limits. The change of scenery could help.

Breaking the silence, Frances said, "Harper, I want to go home. But I want to go to your place, not Patricia's place."

Harper had been so worried about Frances that she hadn't thought about what would happen next. A hospital visit, a psych hold, those would be red flags for Family and Children's Services under normal circumstances. Any leverage she might have had, she lost that day.

A knock on the door distracted them both. Beatriz leaned into the room and said, "Is it okay if I come in?" Her curls were pulled into a loose side braid. Unlike before, she didn't have mascara or lip gloss on. Her face was fresh, like she just woke up and came right there. It seemed plausible as it was only eight o'clock in the morning.

Harper could feel the humiliation rising in her body.

Beatriz trusted her to take care of the children. She expected that Harper would rise to the occasion, but she hadn't.

First, a home inspection. Then a hospital visit. Not only had she failed, she failed so epically that one of the children was hospitalized. Did Beatriz talk with her colleagues about the trainwreck tattoo artist who thought she was capable of caring for two children? Did they talk about all the red flags they missed when approving her kinship arrangement?

"Morning," Harper said.

Beatriz smiled at each of them. "Frances, would you mind if I spoke to you alone for a little bit?"

Frances stared and said nothing.

"I was just going to step out for some coffee. Would you like some?"

Beatriz pulled some change from her purse and said, "Please. Yes."

Harper waved the social worker's hand away and said, "I'll take my time. I have my phone on me, if you need me."

No one stopped her. Frances didn't ask her to stay. They wanted the space to talk about her, her failure, without her around.

Harper didn't linger. She didn't need to hear how she messed things up. Even if they didn't come right out and say it, Harper didn't know if she could deal with the looks or the cautious dance around the truth.

It had been Harper's fault. It had been her fault for not being more forward about her intentions. It had been her fault for not telling the children sooner that she wanted them to stay with her. But if she hadn't told them and they thought she didn't care, the situation could have happened anyway. Every option felt wrong.

An email notification popped up as she waited in line for coffee at the Tim Horton's on the main floor. Harper tapped to open the message from her family lawyer. While Frances slept, she'd messaged him, letting him know what happened. She worried about what he might say.

Dear Harper,

I hope this message finds you well. I have reviewed your email and want to express my sincere concern regarding the situation you and Frances are currently facing. My thoughts are with you both during this difficult time, and I hope you are able to prioritize your well-being and focus on healing.

That said, I must acknowledge that this development has introduced certain complexities, as you have already noted. I will make every effort to manage matters on my end with minimal disruption to you. However, I may need to schedule a brief call with you tomorrow to clarify a few points and ensure we are aligned moving forward.

Please let me know what time would be most convenient for you to connect.

The words 'certain complexities' told Harper everything she needed. This would be the win her mother and Roger needed. One of the last things that Harper could offer that her mother couldn't, stability, had disappeared when they ended up in the hospital on a mental health hold.

CHAPTER TWENTY-SIX

Olive and Levi spotted her at Tim Hortons. Harper had already bought the two coffees and a hot chocolate for Frances. To give Beatriz more time, she sat down. The coffees were starting to cool and she still couldn't bring herself to go back to the room. How could she face Frances when she had failed her?

Levi and Olive took a seat in front of her and asked if she was okay. Harper stared at them and shrugged her shoulders. No words would express the guilt and the worry and the humiliation. Neither of them pushed her to speak, they sat there with her.

"You don't have to stay here with me. You can go up and see Frankie if you'd like," Harper told them.

"We will," Olive said. "But we know she's being taken care of right now. You, you're not."

Harper shook her head and laughed. "I don't need to be. I'll be fine."

Levi bumped her foot under the table. When Harper made eye contact with him, he said, "Be fucking for real. You need some moral support."

She tipped her head in agreement, then reached out and

grabbed both of their hands. She couldn't tell them how much it meant that they were there. Everything had fallen apart. They still showed up.

"Fill us in," Levi told her.

Harper explained what the doctors said, about the stitched, about the email from the lawyer.

"So, what's next?" Olive asked after she finished.

"Beatriz is here. I think this is the end of my time with the kids, at least having them in my custody."

Levi sat up straight.

Olive stared at her, disbelief on her face. "What do you mean?"

Harper raised an eyebrow, surprised they were questioning her. After what happened, a judge would never grant her custody. It clearly wasn't in the children's best interest for Harper to take care of them. She'd done a terrible job. Even her lawyer knew it.

"I hate to state the obvious, but if Frances harmed herself because she thought you were giving her up, wouldn't it mean that she needs you?" Levi asked.

"But that's not a normal reaction. Does it seem healthy that she wants to stay with me this badly? Maybe it's not good for them that I take on that role. Maybe it's crossing a boundary. Maybe it's better if I'm just their sister and nothing more."

"Or," Levi said, "The girl has been passed from one person to the other and you've given her a place to land. You've given her a safe place. You've gotten her a home, an actual home."

Olive gave a 'Mhmm' of agreement.

"I don't think it will matter," Harper told them. "Even the lawyer said it's not looking good."

Levi put both of his hands over Harper's. "Do you still want custody? Like, can you see yourself taking on this challenge for the next eight years, at least."

The kids were in every single version of the future she could see. Even if she didn't have custody, she couldn't imagine life without them. When she thought about things she was excited about, it included things that she and the kids would do together.

"I want to do this."

Olive let out a sigh, obviously relieved.

"Harper," Eddie's voice came from across the wide corridor.

Harper turned in time to see Eddie running toward her, his coat unzipped and a teddy bear in his hand. Patricia, Roger, and his boys walked down the corridor. Roger gave a wave, but Patricia still looked as furious as the day before.

Eddie crashed into her and climbed into her lap as she continued to hug him.

"I brought a teddy bear for Frankie," Eddie said, resting his head on her shoulder.

"She's going to love that," Harper told him.

"You're such a good brother," Olive told him as she reached across to give him a high five. He slapped her palm and nodded.

"Are you coming to see Frances?" Eddie asked Olive and Levi.

Patricia and Roger approached. Kayden and Elijah gave Harper a hug, which she didn't expect. They said they brought candy to give to Frances and asked if they could go give it to her.

Harper nodded. "Why don't we all go see her?"

As a group, they headed toward the elevator. Harper hoped Beatriz wouldn't mind her coffee on the cooler side. Patricia refused to look at Harper, but she spoke to Levi, asking how he was doing, saying how she missed him. She couldn't leave it without mentioning what a good influence he was on Harper. Olive folded her arms in annoyance on Harper's behalf. Levi remained as polite as always.

When they got to the right floor, Harper hung back, letting everyone else enter first. She hadn't realized her mother would do the same thing. They were left behind, forced to acknowledge each other's existence.

"Beatriz says that you haven't retracted your application for custody," Patricia said as they walked down the hallway. She didn't sound angry. The way her eyes widened and the way her lips were relaxed and not tight with anger, Harper wondered if her mother wasn't glad about it.

"I haven't." Harper took a deep breath. "I think it might be a good idea for Frances to get out of the city, away from all these shitty memories."

"No." Patricia took Harper's arm and pulled her to a stop. The rest of their group headed toward Frances' room while she narrowed her gaze at Harper and said, "If you're going to take those kids away, I'm not backing down and this could go on forever depending on what the judge has to say."

Harper raised her eyebrows and said, "So, you're righteous if you fight for them, but I shouldn't? I'm not backing down."

Patricia waved her arms in both directions and said, "Look where we are. Look at what happened. That little girl is lying in a hospital bed and that happened under your watch."

Harper stared at her mother. "Why are you doing this? What are your real motives, because it doesn't seem like it's about the kids. Are you trying to get back at me for something? What are your motives?"

Patricia glared at her. "If you get these kids, you're going to cut me out of your life."

Harper stared at her. She didn't even realize her mother wanted her in her life. Patricia had spent most of Harper's childhood trying to run from the fact that she was a parent, that she had a daughter at home.

"I'm your mother," Patricia said, her voice loud, her entire body tight with tension.

Harper tried to ignore the spark of anger that ignited in her stomach. They were in the hospital after all, but she couldn't act on it as much as she wished she could.

"Listen, my whole life, you've left me to take care of my own shit. You didn't help me with school, or keeping the apartment clean, and you didn't direct me toward my future. You always told your friends how you got so lucky with an independent child, but it wasn't luck. You raised me to need no one. What did you think would happen?"

Patricia tried to cut her off. "I don't think that—"

Harper kept going. "For basically my entire life, I wanted you to help me, to rescue me from all the bullshit, and you did nothing. Now that I might not need you, now that I've decided that I have other people to fill that hole you left, you seem to have a problem with it."

Patricia didn't say anything. Harper had been so prepared for a shouting match that she didn't know what to do with the silence.

"Honestly, if you fight me, you're probably going to win this case. You have your expensive lawyers and all the money you could possibly need to appeal a hundred times over. Those things will crush me in court and I'm not ignorant to that, but I also know I can't let those children think that I gave them up. I'm not going to leave them behind. They need me to prove to them that I will do everything I can for them."

Harper didn't bother to wait around. Nothing her mother could say at that point would matter.

When she got to the room, Eddie and Roger's boys were all on the bed with Frances, eating candy and taking turns making voices for the new stuffed bear. The boys didn't notice she entered the room, but Frances did. She popped a chewy candy into her mouth and smiled at Harper.

Harper smiled back at her.

Beatriz announced that she was leaving, but told Harper

she would be in touch. She glanced around the room and said, "Frances seems to be in good hands for now."

With Roger and Patricia there, it seemed Beatriz was no longer concerned.

Levi inched over and asked, "Are you alright?"

Harper's shoulders rose and fell. She glanced at him and said, "I'm scared of losing them."

He took her hand and linked his fingers between hers. "We'll do everything we can to help you."

With her free hand, Harper wiped a tear from her cheek. When Olive handed her a tissue, she took it.

CHAPTER TWENTY-SEVEN

"Does that sound like a good plan?" the doctor asked Frances as she handed Harper the discharge summary with the prescription to fill once they left.

"What if the medication makes me feel weird?" Frances asked. She flinched a little as she leaned forward to tug the tongue of her shoe.

"It's possible that the first couple weeks you might feel a little unusual. If the side effects are too much or don't go away, we can look into something else that might be a better fit." The doctor sat on the edge of the bed next to Frances and said, "I've given your sister the number for Dr. Pak. Don't be afraid to reach out to your psychiatrist at any time. I want to encourage you to be open and honest about how the medication is making you feel. That can sometimes be hard, but I promise you, it's worth it."

Even six months before, Harper would have scoffed at the doctor's comment about being open and honest. For a long time, it hadn't worked for her. Growing up, keeping her feelings to herself had been a coping mechanism. If she didn't share how she felt, there was no way that people could let her down when they didn't change or when they failed to help.

But hiding her emotions had consequences. She lost Levi. Her relationship with her mother suffered. She had been barrelling toward a lonely existence. If she wanted to be there for Frances and Eddie, if she wanted to maintain her relationships with Olive and Levi, and build a decent co-existence with her mother, she would have to keep being open and honest.

"I'll try," Frances told her doctor.

The doctor gave her a nod and stood up. "It was very nice meeting you, Frances."

Frances tipped her head in response.

Once only Harper and Frances were left in the room, Frances asked, "Are you mad at me for what happened?"

Harper sat forward in the chair. "No. Not at all."

"Before though? Not even for a second?"

Harper braced herself. "I was scared, terrified, and angry at the situation. Ashamed, too. But I wasn't angry at you."

Frances stared down at her hands for a long few seconds. Her chest rose and fell. Harper thought about getting up and hugging her, but didn't want to push it. Frances seemed to be working up to saying something else, so she held back.

When she glanced up, Frances said, "I would get it if you don't want us to live with you anymore. I promise I won't... um..." She touched her leg. "You know. Yeah. I would understand if you want us to live with Patricia."

Harper got up and sat next to Frances. She put an arm around her shoulders and pulled her into her side. "I don't know what's going to happen when we get to court. As much as I want to shield you from that drama, I don't know how I can without making it worse. I want to prepare you for what might happen."

Frances let out a long sigh.

"The judge could take one look at me, our living situation, my tattoos, and my job, and say 'hell no'. Then again, it could go back and forth for a while. We all love you and care about your well-being. We want what's best for you."

"You said that we can say who we want to live with, but do we actually get a say?" Frances asked. Her words were sharp, like she was angry. She had every right to be angry. She was a kid and maybe she wouldn't know what was in her best interest, but Harper understood how she must have felt out of control of her own life.

"You and Eddie will both be meeting with Beatriz the morning before the hearing. She's going to ask you a lot of questions and you're going to have to answer them truthfully."

"I messed things up, didn't I?" Frances asked. "All of this messed it all up."

Harper rested her head against Frances' because she didn't know what to say. The self harm and the hospital visit didn't make things under Harper's supervision look stable, but the blame couldn't be placed on Frances. All the adults in her life failed her, time and again. She didn't need to believe she was at fault for any of it.

"You did nothing wrong. But no matter what happens, I'm going to be right here with you."

CHAPTER TWENTY-EIGHT

THE NIGHT BEFORE THE HEARING, EDDIE AND FRANCES ASKED for the door to the room to be left open. They had been leaving it open more often since Frances' stay in the hospital. Neither of them shut the bathroom door over all the way anymore. It brought Harper a little relief. She stopped closing her bedroom door at night too, so they could come in or call to her if they wanted to.

Harper laid in the dark on the couch, listening to the sounds of Eddie mumbling in his sleep. Having Frances back in the house made her relieved, but also nervous at the same time. Despite the doctors thinking it was safe for her to leave their care, Harper knew emotional wounds weren't an easy fix. Some nights she dragged her duvet into the living room to stay close, to make sure nothing else would happen.

That night, she stayed in the living room to keep them close by, in case that was her last night with them at her place.

When the kids had first showed up at the apartment, Harper couldn't imagine them taking over her space. Giving up her studio had seemed like such a big deal at the time. For some reason, she couldn't imagine herself living without a designated place for her art, but in the dark she opened the listing for the house next to Maz's.

The inside of the house needed work, like the outside, but it was in better shape than she expected. The flooring would need to be replaced and everything would need to be painted, but the roof had been replaced only several years before the owner died. The electrical had been done too. Potential buyers didn't see past the graffiti in the living room and the overgrown lawn.

Harper could see herself moving in there, slowly making changes to fit the aesthetic and the needs of the kids. Three bedrooms, a half-finished basement that could make a decent apartment if she needed to supplement income. She could even give Olive the basement, so she could have a place to stay, to focus on school and not mothering her mother.

The kids could have their own rooms, decorated anyway they wanted. They would have a decent size backyard to play in. Harper could picture them getting a dog like Eddie always wanted. They could live next to Maz and Cassidy. Frances' first job could be babysitting Eaton or cutting lawns. Maz, Cassidy, and Harper could help each other out with the kids and with the properties when necessary.

The amount she was paying for rent would cover all of the mortgage and even the majority of the utilities.

More than all that, she could give the kids a place where they could always feel at home. Even when Frances went off to university or backpacking through Europe. Even when Eddie wanted to move into the basement because he was too cool to share a bedroom wall with his older sister. If Harper had a home for them, they would always have somewhere to come back to.

Even if Patricia and Roger got custody.

The last bit of her savings wouldn't be enough for the down payment. She would have no choice but to ask for help.

She wondered if her mom and Roger would agree to help

her out with the down payment. After everything that had been escalating between her and her mother, it would probably not go over well. Having never asked anyone for money before, she worried how it would make her look in their eyes. Would it make her look weak or useless? Would they use it against her, like 'see, this is why we took the kids from you. You can't even house them'.

A risk, but one she was willing to take. She copied the link and saved it on the notepad on her phone. She decided right then, regardless of the outcome, she would ask Roger if he would help her get a house. Maybe it wouldn't be the house next to Maz, but something smaller, cheaper. She wanted a space that Frances and Eddie would always feel safe in.

A pair of text messages popped up on her phone from Levi.

> Good luck tomorrow.
>
> Get to sleep.

She wished she could tell Levi that she loved him, that she appreciated him. He deserved so much more than she had ever given him and yet she wanted nothing more than for him to give her a second chance. After how it ended, he still wanted the best for her.

As she sent a heart emoji in response, another message came in. Harper tapped on it. From Olive:

> I'm here. Don't wanna wake the kids.
> Come out.

Harper got up, slipped on the socks she'd kicked off, and headed toward the door of her apartment. When she opened it, she found Olive standing in the doorway, wearing a coat over her gas station uniform. She looked exhausted. Her eyelids were half closed as she waved Harper to come out of the apartment.

"What's wrong?" Harper asked, leaving the door open slightly, so she could hear if the kids got up.

Olive sat down on the steps that led to the upstairs apartment. Harper squished in beside her.

"I just wanted to come and wish you good luck tomorrow," she said. Then she yawned.

"Why don't you come inside? You can sleep here. Take over my bed since I'm on the couch anyway," Harper told her.

Olive nodded and said, "Okay, but before we go inside, I'd rather tell you something out here, in case you wanna give me shit about it."

Harper sat up straight. On the night before the hearing, when her future and the futures of the children was at stake, she didn't want any surprises. Her focus needed to be on the kids and not her own issues.

"What is it?" Harper asked, sliding to the side to look at Frances.

Olive pulled out her phone, tapped on the cracked screen a few times, and handed it over to Harper. It looked to be some sort of web-based sales platform and it showed several thousand dollars in sales. Harper handed back the phone and asked, "What is that? Are you selling feet pictures?"

Olive smirked. "I'm not there yet." Then her face went serious again. "This is where you might get mad."

"Fuck. Are you selling *my* feet pics?"

Olive ignored her. "I put together all the art you've done for Eddie to colour in and I made colouring books."

Harper tilted her head, but said nothing.

Olive yawned and went on, "I've been selling colouring books of your drawings for the past month. I created social media pages, a website, and I've been promoting, just to see."

Harper opened her mouth to speak and then went quiet

again. Olive barely had time for herself, but she'd gone out of her way to do that for Harper? It seemed like a terrible decision on her part.

"Why?" Harper asked.

"Because you need the money for the kids and because I wanted to. And I used the website in one of my UX design classes. Kids can colour pages online using a paint feature I created."

Olive shouldn't have done that for her. Olive had so many things on her own plate, she shouldn't have put the energy into something for Harper. Even if it she could get credit for school.

"Don't," Olive warned.

"Don't what?"

"Don't tell me that I shouldn't have done it. Don't tell me to focus on myself. Don't tell me you could do it yourself."

"Well…"

Olive put up her hand and said, "I'm not in the mood for you to argue. Are you going to accept that I did this for you or should I cash this out and shut everything down?"

Harper sat with those words for a few seconds. It bothered her that Olive would go behind her back and do that without her permission. At the same time, she knew she wouldn't have had the time to put something like that together. The idea though, it was great. She wished she'd come up with it herself.

But she didn't have to. Olive had done that for her and she appreciated that even if it made her feel uncomfortable.

"Thank you," Harper said to her, wrapping an arm around her shoulders. "You get a cut."

"Just a onetime cut." Olive laughed. "I'm not maintaining this. I don't have the time, so it's all on you."

Harper squeezed her best friend into her side and said, "Okay, deal. Thank you for helping with this and with the kids. No matter what happens tomorrow, I owe you e—"

Olive cut her off. "You owe me nothing. This is what family does for each other. Like it or not, you're my family."

Harper rested her head against Olive's. "I wouldn't want it any other way."

Olive yawned again.

Harper stood up, dragging Olive up with her. "Come on. Let's get you to bed. We have a big day tomorrow."

CHAPTER TWENTY-NINE

Despite Frances' protests, Olive took her and Eddie out for lunch while Harper, Beatriz, Patricia, and Roger waited for their turn to sit in front of the judge. As they waited to be called in, no one spoke. They sat on hard, wooden benches in a hallway looking at the hanging artwork or the patterns on the marble floor. People came and went in suits and dresses.

Harper hadn't had time to shop for a pantsuit or something to make her look less like herself. She had no choice but to show up in a pair of untorn, unfaded black jeans and a black button-up shirt she'd bought when dressing up as the lead singer of My Chemical Romance for Halloween several years before.

She expected Patricia to say something about her attire, but she sat on the bench a little ways down looking defeated. She barely glanced up from the ground.

When their names were called, the panic really set in. Harper didn't want her mother to see how rattled she was, the way she couldn't catch her breath, so she and her lawyer kept to the back of the group.

They entered the chamber and found a tall, white man standing behind his desk. He pointed at the chairs before turning to his bookshelf and grabbing a manila folder from on top of some law textbooks. The entire wall behind him was bookshelves packed tight. There was a light smell of tobacco in the air, either from the judge himself or whoever had occupied the space before they arrived.

There were leather couches against one wall, away from the desk. Harper's whole body ached from sitting so rigid in the hallway. She wished they would move their conversation to the couches instead.

The judge sat behind his desk. He discussed how things would proceed, how he expected everyone to behave. He made eye contact with Harper when he said he wouldn't tolerate any outbursts, which made her realize the cards were already stacked against her. Patricia might have been still in her seat, but Harper could almost feel her amusement at the situation.

"I've familiarized myself with the case. I've listened to the testimony of Frances and Edward Wilde. All I want to hear right now is why one party should be considered over the other." He cleared his throat. "I understand that this matter has caused some tension, which it often does. For the sake of the children, I would like this to be brief and without future damage to the relationships of everyone in this room. Understood?"

Patricia and Roger said yes out loud. Harper nodded.

The judge tipped his chin at Patricia, Roger, and their lawyer, asking them to go first.

Harper couldn't help but feel that things were already going downhill. Roger sat silent, but Patricia pulled out document after document of proof that she would make a better guardian of the children than Harper. Their lawyer translated a few things that Patricia said into legalese. The judge listened with no expression.

"My daughter does not have post-secondary education

and her work has her occupied on evenings and weekends," Patricia went on.

"Harper Wilde is a tattoo artist, your honour," the lawyer explained for Patricia.

Her mother brought up that Harper liked to drink and party. She spoke of how she lived in a neighbourhood that was undesirable to raise children in. The jabs kept coming, but Harper was surprised to see her mother looked pained to do it. She didn't seem to be happy about trashing her, even though Harper thought she would be revelling in all the details.

Harper's own lawyer touched her arm as if to remind her to stay calm. She bit her tongue to keep from an outburst. The judgement caused her cheeks to burn red. She had come to terms with her flaws in the months since Levi left her and the children arrived, but no one had made such a long-winded critique about everything in her life before.

Her mother thought everything about Harper's life was a failure.

When it was Harper's time to speak, the lawyer handed over all her documents. She didn't make a production out of it the way Patricia had. Her lawyer went over the details of the law, how keeping blood relatives together would be in the children's interest, and how the law should favour children with their relatives. Harper knew it wouldn't be enough.

Then she was asked to speak on her own behalf.

"Nothing in that paperwork is going to make me look great when you put me side by side with Roger and Patricia. My mom is right. I live in a terrible neighbourhood. I don't have a traditional job. I don't make the type of money that they do. But I love these kids. Not just because we share the same DNA. It's only been a handful of months, but I'm learning how to understand what they need and who they are." Harper sucked in a deep breath before going on. "I might not be a perfect parental figure, or sister, or whatever you want to call it, but I'm doing everything I can in order to make sure they're safe and healthy and seen."

"Your mother has raised concerns about your ability to provide a stable environment because of your job. How do you plan to address that?" the judge asked her.

"My version of stability looks very different from Patricia and Roger's. My work will always need me to be there afternoons and weekends. That's the nature of my job. But I think I've still created stability for them. It's just not based on me alone. Frances and Eddie have a community of people who love them and care about their well-being. These same people raised me up and helped me out when I was a kid or a teenager, when I needed someone. Since Frances and Edward have arrived, they have helped me with clothes, babysitting, and talking through the hard stuff that I previously had no experience with. My version of stability is there, but it involves help and a few important people. And despite what's been going on between my mom and I, I would say that for these kids that community involves Roger and Patricia too."

Harper looked at Patricia and Roger. Roger gave her a simple nod. Her mother had turned her full attention to her lap where she folded and unfolded her hands. She didn't look up.

A pang of worry shot through Harper's chest. It occurred to her that no matter the outcome that day, there was a very real possibility that the relationship with her mother would never recover. For years she thought it didn't matter. She thought she'd accepted that her mother would never make the effort that Harper wanted or needed.

Sitting in those chambers made her realize she'd been holding out hope all those years that her mother might put her first, might come to her rescue even once. Had she been pushing everyone else away hoping that Patricia would see that her daughter needed help?

Harper glanced down at her own lap as well, her chest aching. She'd been so childish to think that. It became very clear that whatever hope she'd held on to had disappeared.

"Your mother and the children's case worker mentioned that Frances Wilde had a recent hospital stay? A psychiatric hold," the judge said. "This happened while they were in your care."

"Yes, sir," Harper said.

Her lawyer spoke. "As I'm sure the children's social worker will provide evidence of, Frances Wilde's mental health condition pre-dates Harper Wilde's custody. The stress of losing her father and fear of losing her new home could be the cause."

"Speculation," the judge said. Her lawyer nodded.

"What steps have you taken to take care of Frances' mental health?" the judge asked Harper.

Harper's hands were shaking. If she didn't say the right words, if she fumbled, it would all be over. "It's slow and steady steps. There doesn't seem to be a quick fix, but she has been seeing a therapist every second week, with additional appointments when necessary."

"And from the report from Family and Children's Services it appears she's only now been placed on medication for depression and anxiety?"

Harper nodded. "Yes. It was recommended by the doctor when she was admitted for self harm."

"And may I ask why medication was not brought to the table immediately?" the judge asked.

"I didn't think it fair to force the medication on her. I hoped that with therapy and time either she would improve or we would get to the point that she understood she needed it."

Patricia and Roger's lawyer cleared his throat and said, "It is the job of the guardian to make those decisions and not wait for a child to do so for themselves."

The judge raised his hand to silence him, but Harper knew the damage was done. The lawyer was right. Maybe Harper should have made the call and pushed harder to put her on medication. It might have saved the trip to the hospital. It might have given Frances her confidence back earlier.

Right then and there, Harper knew what the outcome would be. Her mother had been right. She had never been a fit guardian and the children would lose because of it.

"Is there anything else either of you wish to say before I take my time to consider all the information?" the judge asked.

Harper's lawyer looked at her, but Harper shook her head. There was nothing else left. She had failed Frances and Eddie.

Roger said no and thanked the judge.

"Then I ask for some time to review the information. When I have come to a decision, I will call you back into my chambers."

They all rose. Following Roger's example, Harper thanked the judge for his time and left before the rest followed. As expected, Beatriz was called back into the office, likely to provide last-minute feedback to the judge. It wasn't until Harper took a seat on the bench and only Roger and the lawyers sat with her that she realized her mother had stayed back.

Harper dropped her head into her hands. She couldn't imagine what her mother had left to say. All the facts were in and Patricia still couldn't let up. No judge would grant Harper custody after that slaughtering.

CHAPTER THIRTY

"Whatever happens, I hope that we can resume Sunday breakfast," Patricia said to break the silence. Her mother had stayed in the judge's chambers for almost thirty minutes after the rest of them had departed. She looked at no one when she exited, not even Roger.

"Can we talk about this later?" Harper had kept her eyes on the ground, glancing up to check her phone. No one had texted. No one had checked in.

Harper's community was falling apart. The judge had been right. She didn't have the stability to raise two children successfully.

"Are you going to text the children and ask them to come back?" Patricia asked.

Harper had been debating it, but she worried what it would do to them if she couldn't hold it together. When they passed down the ruling, she wouldn't be able to pretend it would be okay. It would ruin her.

"If you want me to, I will," Harper said. She picked up her phone and texted Olive.

> We should be hearing anytime now. Could you bring them back?

The text message switched to read, but she didn't receive a reply. She needed Olive to message her back. She didn't want to be alone when everything she'd worked for proved to be pointless.

"Harper!" Eddie's voice rang out from down the hallway, bouncing off the marble floors. The sound of his excitement made her want to cry.

Olive, Eddie, and Frances weren't alone. Cassidy, with baby Eaton strapped to her chest, walked along next to Noah and Levi. They waved and smiled when she looked at them, but their smiles were hesitant, questioning the status of things.

Harper got up to greet them, catching Eddie as he ran toward her. She scooped him up and gave him a squeeze.

"We brought you a sour cream glazed donut," Frances said, handing her the little brown and red paper bag. Her voice was heavy with sadness.

Harper wrapped an arm around her shoulder and kept her close as she thanked everyone else for coming.

"Maz wanted to be here, but someone had to hold down the fort at the shop," Cassidy explained.

"I appreciate you guys coming. We can use all the support we can get," Harper said, her voice shaking. "I need the support."

"How did it go?" Levi asked.

Harper checked to make sure the children weren't looking at her before making a face that said 'not good'.

The doors to the chambers opened and everyone turned. It got quiet, as if the whole collective stopped breathing in anticipation. Beatriz, who had been down the hallway on the phone, came rushing back, wrapping up her call as she did.

The judge glanced at the new visitors and asked Harper, "Your community?"

She nodded.

"Your community needs to stay here. The rest of you, come in." He smiled at the children and said, "I would like for you to join us as well."

Harper wanted to say that she didn't like that idea. If they were going to get news, she would like to be the one to tell them. She couldn't speak though. She took both of the children's hands.

Her legs were heavy. She could already hear the judge telling her how it wasn't in the children's best interest to entrust her with their care. The job, the neighbourhood, her age, the complete lack of money compared to Patricia and Roger. They were all against her.

They all took their seats, sitting in the same ones they'd occupied before with the exception of her lawyer, who stood and offered Frances the chair next to Harper. Eddie climbed into Harper's lap and rested his head against her shoulder. His quiet suggested he knew the gravity of the situation.

The judge took his time sitting down and preparing himself to address the room. He rolled his chair forward and then backward. Finally, he cleared his throat and said, "There are a lot of times in my job that I worry about what cases like this will do to families, especially ones that are already struggling."

Harper swallowed. Even the judge could see the mess they had created, the divide that had formed. Harper thought she was doing the right thing by fighting, but she had a new fear, that the children would blame her for failing.

"I'm grateful to see how this one turned out," the judge said.

Harper stared at him, confused. When she turned to her mom, Patricia didn't look back. There was no surprise on her face though, like she had been expecting him to say those words. What had she told the judge when she was alone in the chambers? Harper swallowed hard.

Frances reached out and linked her arm with Harper's. Harper tightened her grasp.

The judge patted the folder in front of him, all their paperwork compiled. He smiled and said, "Ms. Wilde, I would have ruled in your favour, as it's what the children wanted."

He used the term 'would have'. Harper held her breath waiting for the 'but'. But she was too poor. But she had friends who looked like hooligans. But she didn't have the bulging wallet.

She'd failed.

"But..." He leaned forward in his chair, putting his elbows on the desk. "I'm glad your mother put all differences aside and dropped her request for custody."

"What?" Harper said, too loud for the space.

"Patricia and Roger are no longer seeking custody."

"Okay. But what does that mean? Are you're granting me custody or..." Harper held her breath.

Eddie and Frances sat up straight, waiting for confirmation.

The judge smiled. "Do you still want it?"

Harper looked at the children. Eddie and Frances looked at her, waiting for her to answer, waiting for her to speak.

"What do you think?" Harper whispered to Eddie while looking at Frances in the chair next to her. "Would you guys like to stay with me? Like, for good?"

When Frances nodded, the dam holding back her tears broke. They rolled down her cheeks. Her breath caught as she tried to control her crying.

In a surprising turn, Eddie started to sob too. Harper squeezed him against her chest and asked, "You want to stay with me, buddy?"

"Yes," Eddie cried into her chest.

Harper grabbed Frances' hand and pulled her close. She looked the judge in the eye and said, "Yes, definitely yes."

Noah announced that they were going back to his place to celebrate. Even Roger, Patricia, and their boys were invited. It took another hour before they left the courthouse, and when they arrived. When Harper, Frances, and Eddie walked through the door, the place erupted into shouts and whistles. Harper couldn't believe her mom and Roger were there with Kayden and Elijah. Eddie, without delay, ran into the middle of the commotion, giving everyone high fives. Frances stuck to Harper's side, smiling and thanking everyone when receiving congratulations.

"Is it too much?" Harper asked Frances when they stopped at the counter to get a drink.

Frances shook her head. "No. I really want to stay."

Harper gave her a side hug and said, "Text Billie and see if she and her mom are free to come by. Your people should be here too."

Frances raised an eyebrow as if confirming. When Harper nodded, she ran off to find a quiet place to make a call.

As she watched her go, Harper noticed that Patricia and Roger were standing in the corner of the living room looking uncomfortable. Elijah and Kayden were off playing with Noah's girls.

Harper had been waiting until they were alone to unleash the questions that had been brewing since the judge made the final call. They both sipped their beer as she approached.

"You don't have to stay if you're uncomfortable," Harper told them. "I can get the boys home if you want to leave them here to hang out."

"That's okay," Roger said. "But thank you for the offer."

"We have to get to know your 'community'," Patricia said. She looked sincere even though her tone was still snarky.

Harper decided not to argue and asked, "Why did you give up?"

Roger took another sip of his beer and stepped back, as if physically giving Patricia the floor to speak.

"It all got so out of hand." She cleared her throat before going on. "And before getting in to it all, I wanted to say something about all your accomplishments. You're right. You did this all on your own or at least without me. You told me before how you had to raise yourself and it made me realize how horrible of a mother I'd been. You didn't accomplish any of this because of how I raised you, but in spite of it."

"Mom," Harper started, but she didn't know how to finish. She had been angry with her mother for a long time. It had informed so much of who she had become, so letting it go wouldn't be easy. Hearing Patricia validate the things she'd been through though, that helped.

"Let me finish." She cleared her throat. "I always thought you were just going through a teenage phase of pushing me away and eventually we would be good. I thought when you were on your own, you might understand why I did what I did."

Harper opened her mouth, but then shut it.

"I thought when I moved to Roger's, when you were on your own, you'd realize you needed me. But you didn't. When you didn't come back, I realized how bad I messed up. You were right to be angry. I haven't been dealing well with that shame."

Harper pressed her lips together to keep from speaking. As much as she wanted to appreciate her mother's moment of self-awareness, it didn't override all the hurt she held on to.

"When I got the call about the kids, when I realized they would be in your life, I thought maybe I could make it up to you. If I took care of your siblings, maybe you would come around more, maybe I could show you I was different. Now, looking back, that was probably painful to see. Roger mentioned be being a parent to someone else might have been triggering."

Harper nodded.

"I just wanted to reconnect with you and I was getting desperate."

Harper ran her hands through her hair. "We could reconnect if you would just send me a happy birthday for fuck sakes." Then she laughed, because it was ridiculous, and such an easy answer.

"I didn't think you'd want to hear from me."

"Of course I did."

"Then I'm sorry," Patricia told her. "I'm a bad communicator."

Harper shrugged. "At least I know I've come by it honestly then."

They smiled at each other.

Patricia picked at the label of her beer bottle and said, "The way you spoke about Frances and Eddie, I could see that they're as good for you as you are for them. You've built a family without me. I think that's part of why I kept fighting, even when you told me you wanted to become their permanent guardian. I think it was jealousy."

Harper stepped forward, about to hug her mom, but she stopped. She didn't even know if her mom liked hugs, if she liked to be touched when she was upset. They'd never gotten to know each other that way.

Patricia didn't know what to do with her hands either. She put one on Harper's shoulder and gave it a squeeze. Then she asked, "Can I ask one favour?"

"Sure," Harper said.

"Can you allow us to help out, to be involved? Nothing forced, nothing the kids don't want to do. I just would like to be in all of your lives and help out where I can."

Harper nodded. "I'd be cool with that."

An awkward silence fell between them. They both needed time to process the intense honesty. Neither of them were used to being so open about it all.

"I think we're going to take the boys and go home," Patricia said after a few seconds.

Roger agreed.

Patricia excused herself to go find Kayden and Elijah.

"I have something for you, but I need you to keep an open mind," Roger told her, keeping his voice low.

Harper arched an eyebrow. "Why are you being so cagey?"

Roger stepped forward and said, "I have some money for you."

"Money?"

He nodded. "Your mother and I have been putting a little money aside for you every month. It's not a lot, but I think it might help you get started on your new life with the kids."

"And my mom is aware that you're telling me about this?" Harper raised an eyebrow.

Roger laughed and nodded. "She planned to tell you, but I think she's hit her emotional limit for the day."

"Fair. But why would you put money aside for me?" Harper asked.

Roger cocked his head to the side as if to say the answer should be obvious. "Your mom wanted to get you out of Green Bridge."

"What if I don't want to get out of Green Bridge?" Harper asked.

"We won't police how you use the money. We put it aside for you. It's yours."

"Good, because I have a plan."

Roger smiled. "What do you have in mind?"

CHAPTER THIRTY-ONE

Maz and Cassidy's house smelled like hot apple cider, the way Harper always assumed houses in Christmas movies smelled. Everyone brought food to contribute to the dinner. Frances and Eddie even baked sugar cookies, though Harper said they were under no obligation to do so.

Maz had dragged a massive tree into the house, which turned out to be so large the star leaned forward, pressed against the ceiling. There were presents shoved under its boughs and stockings for all the kids lined up against the wall. When Harper and the kids arrived, they added to the pile, stacking them up next to the television stand. The small house was filled with people. It made Harper so relaxed to be in their presence.

She stood at the kitchen island packing up the leftovers into containers for everyone. Harper would be dropping her portion at her neighbours' doors when they got back to the apartment. Like most people in Green Bridge, her neighbours were struggling during the holidays. Harper might have been too, if it weren't for the people in that room.

"Want a hand?" Levi asked, setting his beer on the counter between two trays of veggies.

Harper pulled a few containers and lids from their respective stacks and handed them over. "Please, help. Maz and Cass are exhausted, so I wanted to make sure it gets done before everyone leaves for the night."

Levi got to work, following behind Harper as she moved down the counter, filling the container with a little bit of everything.

"You going to see your parents tomorrow?" Harper asked Levi as they got to the end and put the lids on.

"Teyah and I are."

Harper smiled. "So, things are better?"

"It's better. Still lots to work through or try to, but we've got a good system going now. Everyone knows the boundaries and we stick to them," Levi explained as they moved down the line again. "But what about you? Are you guys going to your mom and Roger's?"

Harper nodded. "My mom's picking us up at like seven tomorrow morning. They're going to Roger's parents in the evening, so we're just doing breakfast and presents together. Just the kids and I in the evening."

Harper wouldn't have wanted it any other way.

Olive turned around from where she sat on the couch. "Is your mom still cool about dropping me off at my aunt's place with my stuff in the morning?"

"Definitely."

Lucia, Noah's wife, came into the kitchen and grabbed a green bean that fell onto the counter. She popped it into her mouth before whispering, "Did you tell the kids yet?"

Levi, Olive, and Harper all turned to look across the space. Frances sat with Noah's oldest two, playing some card game they learned in school. Eddie and two kids he'd met that night were learning dance moves, slipping on the hardwood floor.

"We're heading there after I finish packing up everything," Harper said, keeping her voice low. "I asked my mom and Roger if they wanted to be there, since they helped out, but apparently Roger decided against it. Which was a relief, to be honest."

Olive leaned over the couch. "God, I'm sure Patricia didn't take that well."

Harper laughed. "She sure didn't."

Eddie came into the kitchen and leaned against Harper. "Can we go now?" As if to justify his request, he tossed his head back and yawned.

Harper looked at Olive who was still leaning over the back of the couch to watch them.

Olive grinned and said, "I guess it's time."

Harper crouched in front of Eddie and said, "Why don't you and Frances pack up your things and start saying goodbye."

Eddie ran off to get his sister.

Olive looked at Levi and said, "Could I get a ride with you back to Harper's?"

"Of course." Levi turned to Harper and said, "Leave the packing to us. We'll be here, ready to go when you're back."

Harper nodded and mouthed 'thank you'. She reached out and touched his hand. It happened by instinct. Touching Levi always came naturally to her. He gave her a safe place to reach out.

She pulled her hand back and mumbled an apology because even though he'd always been there for her, she didn't know if she could give him what he needed yet. Neither of them needed the heartache again.

He gave her a soft smile and nodded. "Anytime."

Frances and Eddie came over to her, their eyes bloodshot from lack of sleep and too much sugar. They had been busy since early that morning and Harper knew they were ready to go to bed.

They had one more thing to do before that happened.

For the first time that night, Harper had a nervous feeling

in her stomach. She wondered what the kids would think about what she'd done. Would they be able to see what she had in mind or would they be disappointed? It had been a huge decision that she didn't include them in, but more than anything she wanted it to be a surprise.

"We can't leave our gifts," Eddie whined as Harper helped him put his feet into his boots.

"We'll be back to get them," Harper promised, "but there's one thing we need to do before Levi drives us home."

Frances yawned. "Can it wait until tomorrow?"

Harper thought about it for a second. "It could."

"No," Eddie whined. "Now."

Turning to Frances, Harper asked, "Do you want to wait? We can do it on Boxing Day if you're too tired."

Maz strolled over, leaned against the wall, and told the kids, "You wanna go tonight. Trust me."

Frances shrugged. "Okay. Why not."

Maz held the door open as the three of them walked through. Noah shouted, 'Have fun!' from somewhere inside the house. Maz closed the door before anyone said something that might give it away.

It had snowed since they arrived at Maz and Cassidy's. A new layer of fluffy powder lay on top of everything, making the neighbourhood feel still in a way it rarely did. The temperature had dropped, which pushed people inside. Harper tugged Eddie's toque down over his eyes.

The kids hadn't noticed the subtle theme of the gifts from their friends, and Harper appreciated that. Frances hadn't even said anything when she unwrapped the new bedding set, queen size. Harper saw she noticed it wouldn't fit her bed, but was too polite to mention it.

They walked between Maz and Cassidy's empty raised garden beds and headed down the sidewalk toward home. Only inches past Maz's property line Harper stopped and said, "It's up this way."

She walked up the path to the house next door. The kids didn't follow, but stayed on the sidewalk, staring. Harper stepped up the crumbling cement steps and unlocked the front door.

"What are you doing?" Frances hollered at her.

"Going to take a look at our new house," Harper called back. She stepped through the door and switched on the light. The sound of Frances' and Eddie's feet crunching through the snow made her smile.

They ran up the pathway and straight through the door.

"Leave your shoes on," Harper warned them as they stepped inside. "All the flooring has to go."

They didn't wait, taking each other's hands and rushing to explore the place. Harper had been excited when she stepped inside, despite the disgusting carpet that ran through the main floor. She'd pulled up a corner to see solid wood beneath. Noah knew a guy who could sand them down and stain them, even repair the parts that were in bad shape. And he would work for tattoos.

All the walls needed to be painted and the entire kitchen and bathroom needed a renovation, but the inspector said the foundation and roof were good. The electrical had no major issues and with a new water heater, they should be good. She would have to get the windows replaced before the next winter, but Roger and Patricia offered to help, even if Harper only wanted a loan. Interest-free loan only, Roger explained, and Harper hadn't argued.

"Does the fireplace work?" Frances asked, coming back into the living room after exploring. She pointed at the fireplace that someone had painted white.

"Nope. They bricked it off, but I had an idea," Harper pulled out her phone to show her a picture of faux candles lit up in place of an actual fire.

Frances nodded in agreement. "That would be cool."

"Eventually, we can aim to get it fixed, but it'll be low on the priority list," Harper told her. "We gotta get your rooms perfect first."

Frances grinned. "Separate rooms, right?"

Harper nodded.

Eddie ran out and said, "Can we get a dog?"

Harper laughed. "Honestly, I knew this was going to be the first question you asked. We'll see how well you keep your room clean and keep yourself clean, and then next Christmas we can talk about a dog. Does that sound fair?"

"That's so far away," Eddie whined, but it was short lived. He pointed across the room. "What's that?"

Standing against the wall was a tall, thin present wrapped in red and gold striped paper.

"Open it."

Frances and Eddie crossed the room. They tore the paper off in a matter of seconds, revealing the back of a massive frame. Frances grabbed it and turned it around.

In the black picture frame, Harper had used older pictures of Henry Wilde to create a collage of him and the children. In the portrait, Henry sat in a chair with Eddie on his knee. His attention was on Frances, who was laughing. Harper had used pictures that Frances had taken of herself and Eddie to make sure she got all the details right. She had made it as lifelike as she could.

"It's daddy," Eddie said.

"Yeah, and you guys," Harper told him.

"I like it," Frances said in a whisper. There was a pained look on her face.

"My feelings won't be hurt if it makes you uncomfortable. We don't have to put it up or anything if it does."

Frances took the picture and walked across to the fireplace. That had been the spot Harper had picked for it too. It surprised her when Frances turned away and searched for another wall.

"Why not put it up above the fireplace?" Harper asked. "Then you can look at it all the time."

Eddie didn't seem to care about the conversation. He kept staring at the image of his father. Harper wished she could do something more than a picture. Despite her own feelings, despite Henry being a total stranger, she wished she could bring him back for Eddie and Frances.

Frances glanced down at the ground and said, "Because there should be a picture with you up there too. Not just us and dad."

Harper bit the inside of her lips and said, "That's really cool of you to say."

Frances rolled her eyes and said, "Don't get mushy or whatever."

Harper held herself together and said, "Why don't I do the same thing with a picture of the three of us? They can go side by side."

Eddie glanced up. "Yes. All the family."

Frances and Harper looked at each other. They didn't have to say anything else. They understood. Harper wrapped an arm around Frances' shoulders and squeezed her into her side.

"You happy?" Harper whispered.

"I am." Frances glanced up. "Are you?"

Harper let out a laugh. "Definitely."

If you are struggling with self-harm or emotional distress (or you know someone who is), there are resources to help. Reaching out can feel overwhelming, but you deserve support.

Below are just a few of the free, confidential resources where you can talk to someone who cares:

Canada
- Crisis Text Line – Text CONNECT to 686868
- Canadian Mental Health Association (CMHA) – Visit cmha.ca for local resources

United States
- Crisis Text Line – Text HOME to 741741
- Self-Injury Outreach & Support (SIOS) – Visit sioutreach.org for coping tools

United Kingdom
- Harmless – Visit harmless.org.uk for self-harm support and recovery resources

Outside These Countries
- Reaching out to a local mental health organization, your doctor, or trusted community member—you don't have to go through this alone.

Healing isn't linear, and asking for help is a sign of strength, not weakness. Whether you need a listening ear or professional guidance, support is out there without judgment.

ABOUT THE AUTHOR

A.K. Ritchie is an author living in Ontario, where she writes stories inspired by music, travel, and the magic of everyday moments. She has published two books so far; After the Party and Ready to Fall, novels that blend heartfelt emotion with the soundtracks of her characters' lives. Wilde Like Us is her newest novel!

When she isn't writing, you can find her browsing record shops for vinyl, getting lost in the warm colours of autumn leaves, or swaying in the crowd at a live show—always searching for the next story waiting to be told.

To find out more about her and her work:

- facebook.com/AuthorRitchie
- instagram.com/a.k.ritchie
- threads.net/@a.k.ritchie
- bsky.app/profile/akritchie.bsky.social
- amazon.com/author/akrtichie

ALSO BY A.K. RITCHIE

After the Party

Ready to Fall

www.ingramcontent.com/pod-product-compliance
Lightning Source LLC
Chambersburg PA
CBHW020522080526
44583CB00013B/703